MARIA DE PADILLA
QUEEN OF THE SOULS

Humberto Maggi & Verónica Rivas

HADEAN PRESS

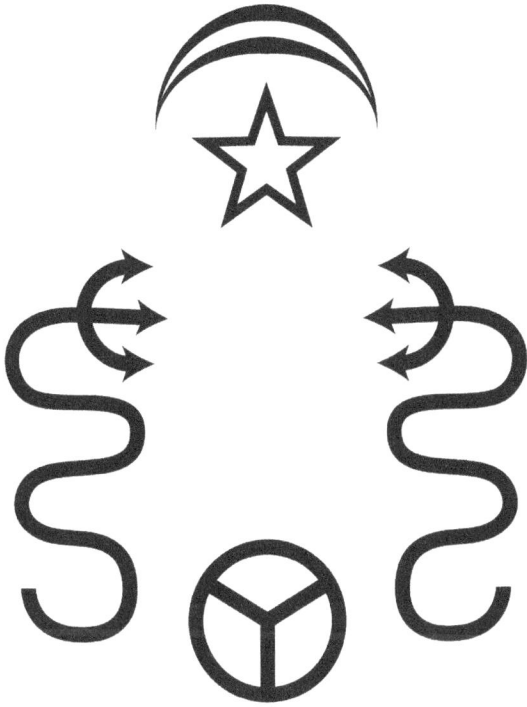

MARIA DE PADILLA

QUEEN OF THE SOULS

CONTENTS

FIRST PART

THE APOTHEOSIS IN HELL

by
HUMBERTO MAGGI

THE QUEEN

Of great importance in the understanding of the sorcery of María de Padilla is the fact, told by History itself, that she was crowned *after her death.*

Necromantic mysteries from the Classical Age tell us that a remarkable life, as much as the circumstances of death, could give rise to two special categories of the dead, the *hero* and the *restless.* Both could be of great help to the sorcerer. Heroes could be worshipped for blessing and protection, and secret information could be obtained by the process of *incubation* - sleeping at the hero's shrine. The restless dead could be invoked to achieve all kinds of magical work, from love binding to receiving favor from judges to winning at the horse's race.

María de Padilla was born in Seville, Spain, in 1334 and died at the age of 27. That would include her in at least one of the categories of the restless dead, the *aoroi* - those who died before their natural time.

The *aoroi* were supposed to be barred from the afterlife at least for the amount of time corresponding to their natural span of life, but the anger and bitterness of unfulfilled expectations could also keep the ghost between the worlds. That would be the case of the *agamoi,* and María de Padilla would fall into this category also, as in life her marriage to King Pedro of Castile was never officially acknowledged, and, although she gave him four children, she could not raise them to adulthood, as the eldest daughter was just seven years old when María died.

While some sources affirm that María de Padilla married Pedro in secret in 1353, in that same year he was forced to marry the French princess Blanche of Bourbon. If the marriage with María truly happened, it was then denied, even though Pedro left Blanche three days after the ceremony and returned to live with María. Although María lived most of the time as the *ipso facto* queen, the supporters of Blanche and very often the Church opposed her presence.

The circumstances of María de Padilla's death in July of 1361 are not clear. The chronicles of Pedro's reign, written by Pero López de Ayala, do not specify the cause of death, only mentioning *su dolencia*, which means some unspecified sickness. As the plague was striking at the time, it has been pointed to as the possible cause. However, Maria died when her only son Alfonso was not yet two years old, and Alfonso himself died shortly after. If he had survived, he would have been next in the succession line, so both deaths were very convenient to the enemies and rivals of Pedro. Some sources accused the king of ordering the execution of Blanche de Bourbon a few months before the death of María, but there is disagreement as to whether Blanche was executed by crossbow or poisoned with herbs. The objective of the execution of Blanche was to confirm María as queen. Regardless, the fact is that María died soon after Blanche and before becoming the queen, and the crown-prince followed in the next year.

María de Padilla was buried three times. The first burial was in the Monastery of Santa Clara de Astusillo, founded in 1353 by María herself. The sin of adultery would have qualified María as a soul sent to Purgatory or even Hell, but Pedro publicly recognized María as his first and only wife one year after her death; the Archbishop of Toledo accepted his reasons and annulled the marriage with Blanche and another marriage Pedro had contracted with a woman named Juana de Castro in 1354. That allowed Pedro to move María's remains to the Royal Chapel inside the Cathedral of Seville, where they were kept undisturbed until 1579, when they were transferred together with other members of the royalty to the crypt under the new Royal Chapel, still inside the cathedral. She rests there together with Pedro and their son Alfonso, inside a wooden sarcophagus lined with red velvet. With them is also buried another son Pedro had with Juana de Castro, named Juan de Castilla, and the half-brother Pedro himself killed, Fadrique Alfonso de Castilla.

We see here the first of the magical-religious reasons that possibly led María de Padilla to become the Queen of the Dead and of the Demons, the *post mortem* coronation itself. Until the moment of her recognition by King Pedro I, orthodox Christian thought would not consider hers a soul capable of any kind of intervention on behalf of the living. On the contrary, she would at best be seen as no more than a needy soul in Purgatory. *Non*-orthodox Christian magical thinking could, of course, see the souls in Purgatory or even in Hell as being exploitable by the sorcerer – just as was done in Classical times. We have several examples of this in the later grimoires; the *Book of Saint Cyprian* printed in Portugal in the end of the 19th century is typical on this matter.

The confirmation of the secret marriage would rectify her *post mortem* status, and the coronation would bestow upon her the sacred powers usually associated with royalty. Throughout the Middle Ages kings were still believed to possess, due to the fact of being chosen by God, powers of healing, exorcism, and fertility. The anointing of the kings and often of the queens linked them to the tradition of sacredness going back to the holy kings of Israel. That would move María de Padilla from the category of the magically exploitable restless dead to a position more akin to another category of the dead, this one typical of orthodox Christian thought: the saint.

The *saint* category came to substitute the old pagan *hero* as being a special kind of dead who had the power to help the living. In the same way heroes had shrines and worship, so did the saints. The important difference here is that the typical saint was created by the very circumstances that were previously believed to give origin to the restless dead. The typical saint was unmarried, preferably a virgin but at least a celibate, went through great sufferings or practiced harsh abstinences, and was often executed for his faith. All that would put the saint simultaneously in the restless categories of *aoroi*, *biothanatoi* (violently executed), *agamoi*, and very often *ataphoi* (not receiving proper burial). The commerce of relics, spreading parts of the corpse all around Europe, would in the classical past have also been seen as having terrible consequences for the departed soul.

The sufferings María de Padilla endured in life, now that her status was not just rectified but raised, could make her the object of devotion. After all, there is a very long list of kings and queens before her who were accepted as saints. The consented burial in the

Cathedral of Seville put her grave in close vicinity with the images and relics adored there. Masses certainly were said inside the vast temple on her behalf, and it is simply to be expected that people would begin to offer prayers to her and, in a second but inevitable moment, would also start to ask for her intercession.

The characteristics of the life of María de Padilla would, of course, make the people expect her to be a blessed soul who would understand and be sympathetic towards amorous problems, and that would probably be the motivation of any woman who approached her sepulcher to offer a prayer and ask for help. According to all the classical necromantic beliefs, these offering of prayers, accompanied almost certainly by the lighting of candles and the making of promises, would be sufficient to further empower her spirit.

María de Padilla's soul would then be well on the path to become a non-official saint, but for one reason.

She was also believed to be a witch.

THE WITCH

It is possible that Maria de Padilla was accused of being an enchantress during her lifetime due to her influence over the king, and that this may have started the legend. It may also be possible that some kind of cult, with candles and prayers, arose at her tomb in the Cathedral of Seville. What is certain is that her name migrated to the spells of folk witchcraft, which are also prodigal of using the names of saints.

One of the oldest magical spells naming Maria de Padilla I have located comes from an *Auto de Fé* of the Inquisition of Lisbon, from the year of 1640:

> "I conjure thee vinegar, pepper and sulphur in the name of so and so, with three from the bakery, three from the cutlery, three from the butchery, three from the yard, three from the weighting, all three. All six, all nine will gather in the heart of so and so, if they are more, or if they are less, 56 devils will gather, in the tower of Primão they will climb nine rods for love they will fetch, in the millstone of Caiphas they will sharpen, in the heart of so and so they will pierce, so he cannot be, or be at rest, until he be with me; Dona Maria de Padilla with all your quadrilha[1] bring me so and so through the air and by the winds; Maria the lost who for the love of a man went to hell, so I ask that you partake of your love with so and so, so he cannot sleep, nor has rest, until he is with me."[2]

---

1. See page 16 regarding the mention of the word quadrilla.

2. *Maria Padilha e toda sua quadrilha*, Marlyse Meyer. The spell is from process 7840 of a witch named Luisa Maria, from the *Auto de Fé* of the year 1640.

Something happened between the death of Maria de Padilla in 1361 and the confession of the Portuguese witch Luisa Maria in the tribunal of the Holy Office (from where the above spell comes) less than three centuries later, that turned the Spanish queen into the mistress of demons, appealed to in a love spell. The keys to this transformation are to be found in her life and in the myths created after her death.

When we come to the *Romancero General*, a series of ballad tales that began to be collected in written form in the 16th century, we see a very different image of María de Padilla. Here she is not the peaceful woman history registered, who tempered the aggressive character of Pedro, convincing him to forgive enemies and who built a monastery with the intention of retiring to live a penitent life. In the *Romancero*, María de Padilla is described as a vindictive *femme fatale* who was behind most of the actions that gained to Pedro the epithet of "the Cruel".

Fundamental to the emergence of the negative image of María de Padilla was the defeat and death of Pedro in 1369, which gave rise to the new and powerful dynasty of the House of Trastámara. The new dynasty began with Enrique II de Castille killing his half-brother Pedro, which probably silenced the poems and ballads where Pedro and María were described in more positive ways. However, the accusations of witchery against María most likely began during her lifetime, spread by the supporters and sympathizers of Blanche of Bourbon. The fascination María exerted over Pedro, making him act against his own political interests, was later attributed to her powers of erotic magic.

Another element that was important in the creation of the myth of the Spanish witch queen was the pro-Jewish policies of Pedro, who was nicknamed "King of the Jews" by Enrique of Trastámara. His treasurer Samuel ha Levi was an important figure in the cohort, and probably inspired the creation in the *Romancero* tales of the character of the Jewish wizard who helped María de Padilla.

The poems in the *Romancero General* are not trustworthy historical sources. One of the most touching of the ballads describes the grief and suffering of María de Padilla when Pedro was killed –

an impossibility since she had passed away many years before. Other poems are clearly fantastic, such as the tale of how María de Padilla asked the Jewish magician to enchant a belt adorned with diamonds Blanche de Bourbon had given to her husband, making it look like a serpent and so estranging Pedro from Blanche. This legend was recently expanded in the Brazilian narratives, where a Kabalistic Jew is presented as having been María's tutor in the magical arts.

Although it is possible that she was involved in the pardon granted to Fadrique Alfonso in 1351, the poems accuse her of asking for his execution in 1358, with an interesting detail:

> *"To what do I owe this, good king*
> *I've never done you any harm*
> *nor left you abandoned in battle*
> *nor left you fighting the Moors.*
> *No sooner has he had his say*
> *when they've cut off his head;*
> *to the lady María de Padilla*
> *they've sent it on a platter...*
> *"Here you shall pay, you traitor*
> *your deeds past and present,*
> *the evil counsel you gave*
> *to King Pedro your brother."*[3]

This passage brings María de Padilla close to Herodias and Salome, accused in the Bible of asking for the beheading of John the Baptist. As it is known, legend has the head of the saint presented to them also on a platter. Herodias later became associated with witchcraft, especially connected with the theme of the night flight through the air.

The Italian form of the name Herodias is *Erodiade*.
It appears that Herodias, the wife of Herod Antipas,
in Christian mythology of the early medieval period

3. *Spanish Women in the Golden Age: Images and Realities*, edited by Magdalena S. Sánchez and Alain Saint-Saës.

came to be seen as a spirit condemned to wander the sky forever, permitted only to rest in treetops between midnight and dawn. By the High Middle Ages, this figure seems to have become attached to the train of nymphs of Diana, now also seen as a host of spirits flying through the night across the Italian countryside. Other names attached to the night flight of Herodias included Minerva and Noctiluca. The Canon Episcopi is a passage from the work *De ecclesiasticis disciplinis* by Regino of Prüm (written ca. 906). It became notable as a paragraph of canon law dealing with witchcraft by the 12th century. Regino reports that there were groups of women who believed that they could go on night journeys where they would fly across the sky to meet Diana and her train. The name of Herodias is not present in the text as attributed to Regino, but in the version by Burchard of Worms, written ca. 1012, the reference to Diana (*cum Diana paganorum dea*) was augmented by "or with Herodias" (*vel cum Herodiade*).[4]

Marlyse Meyer, in her study *Maria Padilha e toda sua quadrilha*, already considered, after the spell from 1640, the connection between the new image of María de Padilla as associated with the medieval theme of the flight of the witches. Here, it is necessary to take a closer look at the term *quadrilla*. In one of the poems of the *Romancero General*, one Payo Rodrigues is accused of treason against the father of King Pedro, for having "entered with a big *quadrilla*" against him together with the King of Portugal. The term thus is related to the idea of a small troop or band, and in the case of the spell seems to indicate that María de Padilla was the head of a small army of spirits. This is a typical description from demonic magic, as in almost every list of spirits to be found in the grimoires we find the mention of how many spirits or legions of spirits a certain demon commands.

---

4. http://en.wikipedia.org/wiki/Cult_of_Herodias

The idea migrated to Quimbanda together with the name of María de Padilha, where we find, besides the term *legion,* inherited from the Roman army, the word *falange,* from the Greek *phalanx,* a Greek rectangular mass military formation of heavy infantry armed with spears, pikes, and other weapons. It is tempting to associate the number of the devils indicated, 56, with the mention made by Plutarch who associated the number with Typhon[5], but given the popular character of the spell it is most probably just a coincidence.

We can identify in this long transformation the same process of apotheosis undertaken by other figures in the past, beginning with the most archetypical of the Queens of Hell, Hecate.

Hecate seems to have started as a rather benign deity in Caria, associated with the protection of liminal spaces and transitions, but by the Roman imperial period, she was raised to the status of a queen of the underworld and as *psychais nekuon meta bakcheuouosa* - "raging among the souls of the dead".[6]

> It was this dominion over restless souls that led to Hecate's familiar role as a magicians' goddess as well, for control of a soul was essential to most ancient magical procedures. Our first hint of this idea comes from a fragment of Sophocles, where Hecate is asked for help in preparing a spell, and from Euripides, whose Medea refers to Hecate as the goddess who dwells close to her hearth. Later, Horace's dreadful witches demand that Hecate help them to invoke the souls of the dead, and she frequently is asked by magicians of the imperial age to help them gain control of aoroi and biaiothanatoi - the souls of those who have died before their time or violently.[7]

---

5. Plutarch, *Moralia* V:30

6. *Restless Dead*, Sarah Iles Johnston.

7. *Restless Dead*, Sarah Iles Johnston.

Even more significant to our comparison is the fact that at least two myths about the origins of Hecate say that she started the apotheotic process as *a human restless soul*. In the earliest attested version of Iphigenia's myth, after being sacrificed by her own father to appease the goddess Artemis, Artemis herself caused her to "become Hecate". Another version mentions an anonymous rude woman of Ephesus who offended Artemis and was first changed by the goddess into a bitch, but when changed back felt so ashamed that she hanged herself – a form of suicide traditionally linked to virgins. Artemis then adorned the corpse with her own clothing and jewellery and "named her Hecate".[8]

Hecate is not the only example of this apotheotic pattern we see repeated in the evolution of María de Padilla. In some versions of their myths, both Naamah and Lilith began as human figures who later gave their names to queens of Hell. Naamah is an obscure woman named in Genesis 4:22 as being a descendant of Cain, and is later identified in Midrash as the wife of Noah. Being of Cain's blood was already enough to raise connections with witchcraft, and in the *Zohar* of the 13th century the name passed to one of the four queens of Hell, the Mother of Divination and one of the four demons of sacred prostitution who mated with the fallen archangel Samael. One of the other four queens is Lilith, who also in some versions was a female human, the first wife of Adam – before leaving him and giving birth to innumerable hosts of demons. She also most likely began her career as a lesser deity or daemon in Sumer until she was raised to the post of underworld queen.

The truth is that there is an archetypical place for a Queen of the Underworld as much as there is one for the Queen of Heaven. The concession of the Church to a place of prominence for the Virgin Mary – initially a secondary character in the narrative of the Gospels – and the slow emergence of another María as Queen of Hell points to the fact that this mythological *loci* sooner or later will be filled.

---

8. *Restless Dead*, Sarah Iles Johnston.

The Queen of Hell's natural province is the control of spirits (the demons and the dead), which are traditionally associated with all kinds of spells. That connects her with the witch, a figure that goes very far into the past, with roots much older than Christianity. The witch was already seen with dread and suspicion during the Greek-Roman age, when she was usually associated with necromancy and the underworld gods, like Hecate, Persephone, and Hades; but if we want to find the witch's origins we must look at the primitive societies of pre-agrarian times.

The craft of the witch is inherited from the shaman, but in the transition to cosmopolitan cultures, the traditional role of the shaman passed to the priest class and the witch became rogue. This is clearly seen in the Mesopotamian cities, where unnamed witches are listed in the tablets of the state exorcists as being a constant source of danger.

Although the study of the Mesopotamian tablets point to a culture plagued with witch fear, the absence of trials and punishments is remarkable, especially when compared to Europe during the height of the great witch hunts. The difference arises from the fact that Mesopotamian legislation put the onus of proof on the accuser, and the accuser was subjected to the same penalties the accused was supposed to face, if he could not prove his claims. Mesopotamians usually preferred to fight witchery on its own terms.

There is a direct line between the Mesopotamian methods of witchcraft and anti-witchcraft and the methods to be found in the late Iberian cultures, where Maria de Padilla began her career as the Queen of the Witchcraft; this is easily noted when we compare some of the magical secrets of the Portuguese *Book of Saint Cyprian* with the magical tablets. These practices became widespread in the Mediterranean basin during the time of the Greek and Roman conquests.

The Greek-Roman cultures resented the introduction and diffusion of this witch lore, as we see in the very harsh legislations put in place against it. Classical writers created an exaggerated image of the witch as a foreign woman whose powers were generally more harmful than benefic. The foundational character of this traditional figure is Circe, a minor deity of magic and witchcraft that in some sources is described as a daughter of Hecate. Circe teaches Odysseus the necromantic craft, enabling him to successfully invoke the ghost of the prophet Tiresias. Other witches from the Latin literature are always connected with necromantic practices, such as Canidia, Sagana, Erichto, Meroe, and Panthia, but all the classical witches lacked a special feature which would appear only later, around the 15th century: the connection with the Devil through the *pact*, the *mark*, and the *Sabbath*.

The diabolical witch arose in the trials that occurred in two valleys south of the Rhone, in France, which began in 1428.[9] The emergence of this new character attests to a change in the way the relationship between humans and demons was defined. After Saint Augustine, the demons were defined as treacherous helpers and teachers of the magicians, whom they deluded into perdition while at the same time tricking them into evil works. Christian magicians tried to bend the paradigm, defending a system of magic where God and the angels helped the magician to subdue and force the demons to their will.

But from the 15th century onward the Church became obsessed with the idea of a conspiracy movement headed by the Devil and aided by the witches. The relationship of these witches with their "god" was not disrespectful and abusive (as with the Christian magicians), and neither were they temporary in a specific ritual context (like with the Classical witches): the diabolical witches were believed to sign a pact and join the infernal retinue under the bond of permanent obedience and vassalage. They became soldiers in the war against Heaven, and the Devil put on each of them a mark.

The legend of the Padilla witch has its origin in a century prior to the rise of the diabolical witch but, as we will see, became inextricably linked with it.

---

9. *Europe's Inner Demons*, Norman Cohn.

Pombagira

The tradition of folk witchcraft from Portugal, which adopted the Spanish spells where the name of Maria de Padilla was found, soon migrated to the New World. The Holy Office used to punish witches with exile to colonies such as Angola and Brazil, and there they began the process of hybridization with the Native American and African traditions.

> Another specific feature of colonial witchcraft, which began to accentuate in the end of the XVI century, was its association to the African magical practices. According to the Visitations [of the Inquisition] in Bahia, a slave from Guinea named André Buçal made divinations with pans and boilers around 1587. Since then, the references grow: around 1610, the witch Maria Barbosa, protégé of the governor of Bahia Don Diogo de Menezes, acted in collusion with the negro Cucana, who made powders with scraps from certain roots. In 1616, white men already used the knowledge of the black sorcerers to get the cure to relatives and friends.[10]

> In 1767, in the river Tajurá, many people – the majority Native American – used to make sorcery operations invoking the demon, pretending to make spirits descend, prophesying future things and discovering the hidden ones, pretending, by those means, to cure and heal the sick. All the cases refer to a very similar practice. Ludovina Ferreira, white woman, assimilated the curative magic of

---

10. *Inferno Atlântico, Demonologia e Colonização nos Séculos XVI-XVIII*, Laura de Mello e Souza.

the indigenous people; around 1735 she promoted cures in the company of the native American Antonio.[11]

It is in this context that we see the name of Maria Padilha appear in Brazil at the beginning of the 18th century. In 1713 the Holy Office exiled the Portuguese witch Antonia Maria to Angola, but she ended up in Brazil where she would relapse and be prosecuted again. The name of Maria Padilha appeared in her spells, and in fact became so popular it caught the attention of the historians:

> Among the magical and sorcery practices transmigrated to the colonial lands and which suffered significant alterations, we must at last allude to the orisons invoking Maria Padilha. There are four cases of this kind of orison among the processes we are now studying [Inquisition processes], and there is information about tens of them in the 17th century Brazil, associated always to other elements of the orisons of conjuration. Even today, Maria Padilha is to be found among us Brazilians. In the Umbanda, syncretic form of popular religiosity which incorporates the Catholicism, the African religions, the native American religions and Kardecism, Maria Padilha is Pombagira, that means, one of the spirits which possess the persons who frequent these rituals.[12]

These conjure orisons indicate some of the main contributions inherited by Quimbanda from the folk witchcraft practiced in Portugal. These spells presented a necromantic understanding at odds with the official demonology of the Church. In these heretical

---

11. *O Diabo e a Terra de Santa Cruz*, Laura de Mello e Souza.

12. *Inferno Atlântico, Demonologia e Colonização nos Séculos XVI-XVIII*, Laura de Mello e Souza.

views, the Devil is at the head of an army composed both by demons and by dead human souls, and, most importantly, *those demons have wives*. If we go a little further, we see this feature also present in the original Spanish spells later adopted by the witches of Portugal, as seen in this spell from the Holy Office of Valencia in 1655:

> *I conjure you*
> *By the lady Maria de Padilla*
> *With all her quadrilla*
> *By the Marquis of Villena*
> *With all his people*
> *By the wife of Satanas*
> *By the wife of Barrabas*
> *By the wife of Belcebu*[13]

Along with the wives of Satanas and other demons, who are mentioned in many spells but are not identified by name, there are a number of named female dead souls who also appear in these spells. Maria Padilha figures preeminently, but we also have figures like Maria da Calha, Marta the Lost, and the mother of Saint Peter, the last being recognized in some spells as "the greatest she-devil who art in hell and brings the broth to the hanged".[14] The folk magical vision differs from the orthodox as it presents the idea that human souls can, after death, assume positions of command in the infernal armies, becoming powerful intercessors and helpers of the witch.

We cannot stress enough the danger this view presented to the Church, as it attacked the foundations of Christian eschatology and undermined its main threat, the promise of eternal punishment after death. Curiously, there are registers in the processes of Inquisition where the fear of the punishment in Hell was the alleged reason for people making pacts with the Devil.[15]

We see that the Portuguese witchcraft heavily influenced the

---

13. *La Inquisicion y los gitanos*, Maria Helena. Sanchez Ortega.

14. *O Imaginário da Magia*, Francisco Bethencourt.

15. *Religion and the Decline of Magic*, Keith Thomas.

aesthetics of Quimbanda. There is no doubt to anyone who sees the iconography of Exus and Pombagiras that their appearance matches perfectly old fashioned ideas about how the Devil appeared. Here we find the horns, the tails, the hoofed feet, tridents and skulls and fire. The bare-breasted statues of Pombagiras take us back directly to the descriptions of how some Portuguese witches used to invoke the devils, also bare-breasted and with the hair loose or disheveled.[16]

From the Portuguese witchcraft also came the notions of an infernal hierarchy. Already in a process of the Inquisition in Lisbon in 1559 we find the title *Maioral* given to the Devil as the head of cults and of Hell.

> The food, [she] said and confessed, stinks of sulfur and pitch; and on the table were for light some torches with cables of cords drenched in pitch which gave a dark, obscure and stinking illumination. And at the head of the table was seated her Maioral in his chair with back support, with a long cloth like a curled hood, and, sometimes, he had it [the hair] cropped and a very long beard; and as a King they adored and obeyed him and served him on their knees and on the table many others of that malign spirits served.[17]

Maioral (1. the head, chief, boss, big shot. 2. *fig* the largest, biggest, greatest[18]) became the name or the title of the leader of the legions and phalanx of Quimbanda. In a second moment of European influence, Aluizio Fontenelle, in 1951, published his book *Exu* where a direct connection is created between the Exus of Umbanda with the spirits of the 18th century grimoire, *Grimorium Verum:*

---

16. *Inferno Atlântico, Demonologia e Colonização nos Séculos XVI-XVIII,* Laura de Mello e Souza. Maria Helena Sanchez Ortega in *La Inquisicion y los gitanos* also mentions a spell which the witches had to be totally naked and with loose hair to perform.

17. *Feiticeiro, profetas e visionários,* Yvonne Cunha Rêgo.

18. http://michaelis.uol.com.br/moderno/ingles/definicao/portugues-ingles/maioral_568519.html, *Dicionário de Inglés Online,* Michaelis.

... the supreme entity of the "left" is the Devil Maioral, or Exu Shadow, who only very rarely manifests in ritual trance. He has as generals: Exu Marabô or devil Put Satanaika, Exu Mango Tree or devil Agalieraps, Exu-Mor or devil Belzebu, Exu King of the Seven Crossroads or devil Astaroth, Exu Tranca Rua or devil Tarchimache, Exu Veludo or devil Sagathana, Exu Tiriri or devil Fleuruty, Exu of the Rivers or devil Nesbirus and Exu Calunga or devil Syrach. Under the orders of these and commanding others more are: Exu Ventania or devil Baechard, Exu Quebra Galho or devil Frismost, Exu of the Seven Crosses or devil Merifild, Exu Tronqueira or devil Clistheret, Exu of the Seven Dusts or devil Silcharde, Exu Gira Mundo or devil Segal, Exu from the Woods or devil Hicpacth, Exu das Pedras or devil Humots, Exu dos Cemitérios or devil Frucissière, Exu Morcego or devil Guland, Exu das Sete Portas or devil Sugat, Exu da Pedra Negra or devil Claunech, Exu da Capa Preta or devil Musigin, Exu Marabá or devil Huictogaras, and Exu-Mulher [Exu-Woman], Exu Pombagira, simply Pombagira or devil Klepoth. But here are also the Exus who work under the orders of the orishá Omulu, the lord of the cemeteries, and his assistants Exu Caveira [Exu Skull] or devil Sergulath, and Exu da Meia-Noite [Exu of Midnight] or devil Hael, whose more well known names are Exu Tata Caveira [Exu Tata Skull] (Proculo), Exu Brasa [Exu Flame] (Haristum) Exu Mirim (Serguth), Exu Pemba (Brulefer) and Exu Pagão [Pagan Exu] or devil Bucons.[19]

In these hybrid schemes, the *Maioral* assumes a position above the three chiefs from the *Grimorium Verum*, who in their turn assume a leading place between the Maioral and the rest of the retinue with

---

19. *Exu*, Aluizio Fontenelle.

more typical names. This second moment of influence of European magic in the formation of Quimbanda is aptly indicated by Bastides, describing the intellectual milieu where Quimbanda developed in the beginnings of the 20th century:

> The spiritism is frequently more or less mixed with the occultism and the black men with instruction, with the aim of showing their science, did not stop reading the books of astrology, of alchemy or of the secret sciences to be found in the libraries of Rio [de Janeiro]. As did the white men, who were the chiefs of the spiritism of Umbanda.[20]

---

20. *Immigration et métamorphose d'um Dieu*, Roger Bastide.

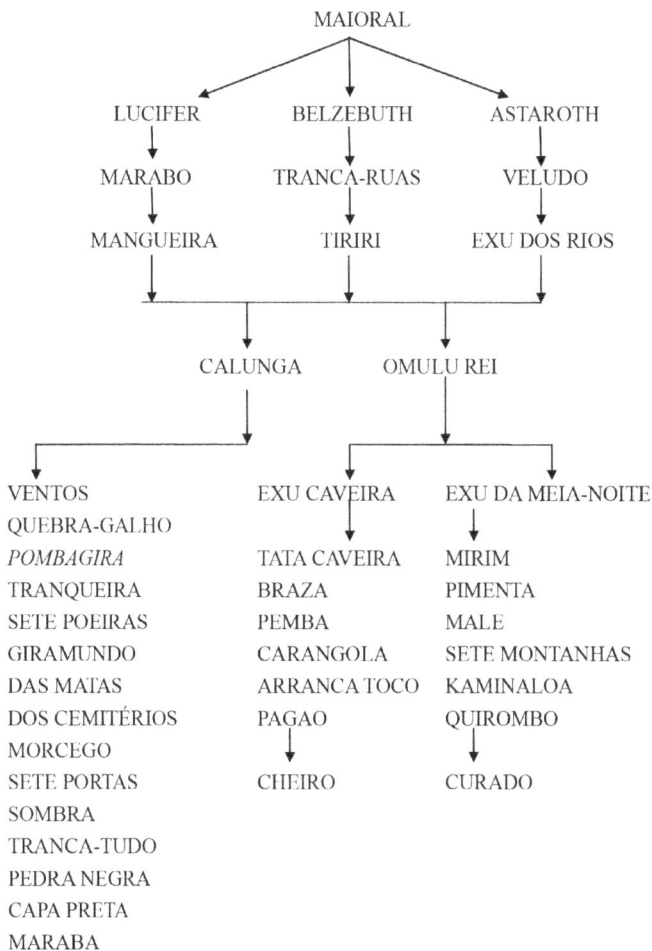

MAIORAL

LUCIFER   BELZEBUTH   ASTAROTH

MARABO   TRANCA-RUAS   VELUDO

MANGUEIRA   TIRIRI   EXU DOS RIOS

CALUNGA   OMULU REI

VENTOS
QUEBRA-GALHO
POMBAGIRA
TRANQUEIRA
SETE POEIRAS
GIRAMUNDO
DAS MATAS
DOS CEMITÉRIOS
MORCEGO
SETE PORTAS
SOMBRA
TRANCA-TUDO
PEDRA NEGRA
CAPA PRETA
MARABA

EXU CAVEIRA

TATA CAVEIRA
BRAZA
PEMBA
CARANGOLA
ARRANCA TOCO
PAGAO

CHEIRO

EXU DA MEIA-NOITE

MIRIM
PIMENTA
MALE
SETE MONTANHAS
KAMINALOA
QUIROMBO

CURADO

Calundu, Cabula, and Macumba

The methodology of folk Portuguese witchcraft seems very simple when compared to the grimoires of ceremonial magic, and one of the reasons I identify as an explantion is the different degree of *familiarity* the common people had with the demons and spirits. Grimoire magic tended more and more to view the spirits as dangerous and treacherous entities, inspired by the Augustinian view which described all of them as fallen angels engaged in an eternal war against God and men. However, the common people often resorted to them in search of relief for the harsh conditions in which they lived; the conditions around them, together with their simplicity of mind and lack of higher education, demanded simple and direct ways to resort to magical help. The idea of the demonic pact of the witch, heavily imposed by the Church, also helped to create the idea of a familiarity with the Devil. After all, the pact and allegiance with the Devil made obsolete the concerns with all the purifying and preparatory measures preached by the grimoires; the demons were now seen as friends, lovers, and protectors of the witches. Ironically, once again, the mystifications of the inquisitors helped to create (or to revive) other ways of magical communion.

> The Inquisition ferreted devils out in the colonial world, seeing them many times where they were not. But, in an intense way, the men in the first colonial centuries shared their quotidian lives with devils, little devils, and the like. Even when they knew the resource to them was illicit, they could not help invoking them all the time. [...] during the 16th, and still in the 17th, centuries they populated the day-to-day of each one, like they were domestic and almost harmless deities. At least, the understanding the colonists had about them differed much from the one the demonologists delineated in their treatises

and became the cornerstone of the inquisitorial procedures.[21]

The repulsive and often terrifying appearance did not hinder, however, that the devil was frequently beseeched and invoked in conjurations. In the colonial period, it seems to have been very frequent the resource to the demoniacal forces. Many women boasted of talking to demons, invoking them, and walking with them in great danger [...][22]

This is another very important feature passed on to Quimbanda. The adept of Quimbanda must make pacts and deals with the spirits, some more general and some more specific, and develops a very close relationship with one or more Exus and Pombagiras who act as his or her counselors, teachers and protectors, thus repeating the same pattern the inquisitors of the Church tried so hard to expose in the confessions.

The spells recorded by the Holy Office usually indicated short and simple magical actions accompanied by equally short and simple conjurations, but it was an enhanced and much more powerful method Quimbanda would receive from the African traditions, and its method remained extraordinarily consistent throughout more than 200 years. We can already identify the main features of a typical Quimbanda ceremony in the descriptions given at the beginning of the 18th century to the *calundus*, meetings where the use of instruments of percussion and music prepared the participants for ritual possession:

> [He] knew closely the calundus, probably went as far as frequenting them [...] knew that they were parties very frequent in the city of Bahia and its surroundings; at them, the black people jumped a lot, made many

---

21. *O Diabo e a Terra de Santa Cruz*, Laura de Mello e Souza.
22. *O Diabo e a Terra de Santa Cruz*, Laura de Mello e Souza.

grimaces with the body and screamed until falling on the ground as dead. "They stayed like that for a time, and when they got up, they said that the souls of their relatives came to talk" during the time they were unconscious.[23]

Here we see a method founded upon *trance possession* used to open communication with the spirits of the dead. Of course, the Augustinian theology of the Church would deny the participation of the ancestors and accuse the spirit of being a liar devil. Europe did know, of course, of the phenomenon of possession, but dealt with it in the most extremely negative way. The trance possessions practiced after African teachings, however, were seen as the fundamental method of communion with deities and ancestors and the way these could directly interact and protect the people. We can see the similarities between the above description of the possession in the Calundu of the 18th century and the Cabula and Macumba of the 19th century.

> "[...] after the first *nimbu* [invocatory chant in the Cabula ritual], the *embanda* [the main priest] went into a trance state, [...] in that moment "the *embanda* [began to have] contortions, turning the eyes [making] grimaces, [struck] the chest with the closed fists and, rhythmically, emitting deep roars, [giving], at last, a strident scream, horrible." This is the observable phenomenology in many initiated in the Macumba, who believed themselves to be 'possessed' by the spirits of depraved men, according to the metamorphosis made in the *terreiros* [meeting places] of Macumba, under the influence of the Kardecist Spiritism, over the mythical phallic orisha and messenger of the other orishas, Exu.[24]

---

23. *O Diabo e a Terra de Santa Cruz*, Laura de Mello e Souza.

24. *Cabula e macumba*, Valdeli Carvalho da Costa. Published in the

The descriptions of the present giras of Quimbanda show that their most likely line of descent is through the Cabula and the Macumba. The ritual of the Cabula was registered at the end of the 19th century by a Catholic bishop, and presented striking similarities with the Macumba practiced in Rio de Janeiro, registered at the beginning of the 20th century, principally in Rio de Janeiro, which in its turn gave rise to Quimbanda. Valdeli Carvalho da Costa[25] presented a detailed comparison of the similarities between the two, Cabula and Macumba, of which we must highlight the following:

1. In the Cabula were used Cabalistic signs like the Sign of Solomon, crosses, together with lighted candles. The use of these symbols already had a very ancient history in Brazil's syncretic folk magic. In the Macumba, the *ponto-riscado*, a series of symbols usually drawn inside a circle which represent a specific deity, were drawn on the floor, as a signature which confirmed the identity of the spirit possessing the priest, and were composed with the Sign of Solomon, crosses, moons, five-pointed stars, arrows, rays, etc.
2. In the Cabula and the Macumba the possessing spirits received cigars and alcoholic drinks.
3. In both, the priests possessed by the spirits danced. In the Cabula the ceremonial meeting was called *engira*, which probably is the origin of the current Quimbanda word *gira*, which by its similarity with the Portuguese verb *girar* (turn around) aptly describe the rite where the possessed people dance turning around and following a circular path.
4. The Cabula had a practice to help the initiate find a personal "spiritual protector", a practice continued in the Macumba and in the Quimbanda.

The other fundamental component of the method of

magazine *Síntese* n° 41 (1987).
    25. *Cabula e macumba*, Valdeli Carvalho da Costa. Published in the magazine *Síntese* n° 41 (1987).

Quimbanda, also inherited from the African traditions, is the *offerings* made to the spirits. The concept of offerings had disappeared from the grimoires since the *Hygromanteia*[26], where we still found peeled fruits being offered to the black demon Mortze, and an offering to the "Lady of the Mountains" which must closely resemble current offerings to Pombagira:

> At the first of August put honey and pine kernels in a bowl, take various colored silken pieces of cloth and write the following words on a parchment: Linomo, Kouoro. Take all these things and go to a mountain at the same day, place them on a firm rock at noon and hide.[27]

It was an ancient concept also present in the Greek magical papyri[28] from the 2nd-5th centuries, which disappeared due to its association with the Augustinian accusations of idolatry. Of course, Portuguese folk witchcraft did not have to follow the Church doctrine, and we find some simple examples of offerings:

> In the great arsenal of orisons she used, Antonia Maria, the witch from Recife, possessed some which were demonized. To bind the lover, she cut a she-goat cheese in three portions, and, putting them in the window, between the nine and ten of night, said: *This little cheese we want the first piece to Barrabas, the second to Satanaz, the third to Caifas, that all three want to gather immediately, and what we ask they want to grant, that so and so came to take us and through the door he will enter, and that he cannot be without us.*

26. *The Magical Treatise of Solomon or Hygromanteia*, translated and edited by Ioannis Marathakis.

27. *The Magical Treatise of Solomon or Hygromanteia*, translated and edited by Ioannis Marathakis.

28. *The Greek Magical Papyri in Translation, Including the Demotic Spells*, edited by Hans Dieter Betz.

The witch participating by pact in a devotional alliance with the Devil was expected to honor her master with deeds, aimed to spread the devilish influence in the world and to increase the satanic following. African traditions also participated in the idea that the deities and the ancestors required a permanent cultic devotion. Both views were married in Quimbanda, where the Exus and Pombagiras must receive both permanent and specific offerings *and* must be helped in their missions amongst men by the mediums with whom they are associated.

Spiritism and Umbanda

The doctrines of Allan Kardec arrived in Brazil around 1845 and quickly became very popular with the middle class, receiving a high degree of social acceptance. This created a situation of contrast with practices like the Macumba, which were then dubbed "lower spiritism". Whilst Spiritism, following Kardec lines, was viewed as a scientific and moral enterprise, "lower spiritism" suffered a strong persecution from the police.

A compromise solution arose in the first decades of the 20th century with the creation of Umbanda. We know that the three main kinds of spirits typical of Umbanda, the Old Blacks (Old Black Slaves), the Caboclos (Native Brazilians), and Exus were already known then, because Umbanda was specifically developed to give the Old Blacks and the Caboclos an acceptable place to work. These spirits came from the Macumba and other forms of "lower spiritism" and, although manifesting now and then in the Kardecist mediumistic meetings, were there treated as inferior and not allowed to fulfill any significant role.

The influence of Kardecism was decisive in the formation of the actual view of the Exus and Pombagiras. Kardecism defends concepts that became central to the actual view of the Quimbanda, like reincarnation and the evolution of the soul, and proposes a simple view of the spirits where the theological distinctions between dead souls, angels, and demons disappear: angels are just purified and evolved souls, and demons are souls degraded into perversions and wickedness.

That led to negative interpretations of the traditional African way of trance possession and a more difficult compromise to include the Exus and Pombagiras, who gradually were reinterpreted as the souls of dead magicians and witches, specialists in magic and sorcery who now work to better their spiritual state and pay karmic debts.

THE DEVIL AND THE ORISHA

However, it was not just the demonological ideas of folk Portuguese witchcraft that contributed to the creation of the concept of the Exus and Pombagiras of Umbanda and Quimbanda. As the names of their categories themselves indicate, fundamental features of the nature and function of these spirits came from the African deity *Esù*.

Esù is an *orisha* or *ebora*, a deity in the Yoruba religion, created by the transcendent creator *Olodumare* to fulfill the fundamental task of ruling the *dynamis* of the universe. This is the reason why, whilst other orishas rule and are responsible for one specific part of or action in the world, like the rivers, the rain, war, and death, Esù's influence and responsibility is omnipresent; he is the orisha of movement and consequently of change itself.

> In fact, Esù is not related only to the feminine and masculine ancestors and their collective representations, but he is also a constitutive element, not of only the supernatural beings, but also of everything that exists.[29]

The concept of being ever-present in movement and change and so associated with the growth and multiplication of everything led to the idea of the multiplicity of individual Esùs. Every orisha, for instance, has his Esù, understood primarily as his individual dynamis *but* he also has a specific name, a kind of individuality and must always be propitiated first with offerings.

---

29. *Os Nago e a Morte*, Juana Elbein dos Santos.

Olodumare[30] created Esù as an entirely special ebora in such a way he must exist in everything and reside in each person. By virtue of his competency and power of realization, of his intelligence and dynamic nature, the Esù of each one must direct all his ways in life.[31]

Esù accumulates other functions, being the orisha of communication and the intermediary between the worlds, between men and the deities. He rules the ways, being able to create, to open, and to close them. He is by consequence the one who carries the offerings, and so is responsible for inspecting and controlling the sacrifices – he will not for instance carry an offering not correctly prepared.

> Esù is the *restorer principle* in the Nago. He is the rigid controller of all sacrifices. General inspector, [...] "impartial police officer" [...] the action of esù is ... to punish the transgressors, particularly the ones who neglect to do the prescribed sacrifice.[32]

Herein lies the frightening aspects of Esù, the deity responsible for correcting the paths and capable of everything to achieve that. Esù in the African myths has an undeniable trickster quality, which he uses to achieve his aims. But we are outside the Christian conceptions of good and evil when treating about not just Esù, but also all other orishas and eboras who are basically beyond these concepts.

This was one of the elements that lead to the identification made between Esù and the Devil, a process already begun in Africa by the Church. It is important to notice that this association came from "the outside"; when identifying the orishas with the Catholic

---

30. The higher deity, creator of everything, but a *deus absconditus* who delegated the governing of the world to the orishas.

31. *Os Nago e a Morte*, Juana Elbein dos Santos.

32. *Os Nago e a Morte*, Juana Elbein dos Santos.

saints in the New World, the insiders of the cults associated Esù with saints like Saint Anthony and Saint Peter, but missionaries in Africa of course had to see things in a very different way.[33]

The other important element in the association Esù-Devil was sexuality. From the rule of Esù over movement and growth, is not difficult to see why he was also associated with sex and procreation, being represented very often with phallic images. Sex was already associated in Europe as being a province of the Devil, and an important amount of magical practices dealt with love and sex. Other iconographic associations between Esù and the Devil were also easily made: in Africa Esù, as was the Devil in Europe, was associated with fire and the colors black and red.

> The first publications making reference to Exu Elegbará in Africa already showed the tendency to identify it with the devil of the Christians in reason of his not very conventional public places and offerings and his ecstatic manifestations in the body of his priests. The same brothers Lander [1832] described the behavior of a priest possessed by Exu as "with frenetic air and roaring like he was possessed by a malign spirit."[34]

This is an important description for us, as it connects the ceremonial methods of possession we already saw to its African roots.

The precedence of Esù in every ritual and offering highlighted his importance to what in the Christian view could only be magical ceremonies, as Europeans denied the status of religion to the African beliefs. The obsession of the Inquisition with the concepts

---

33. According to P. Adelumo D'pamu, "In Niger the identification of Exu with the demon became more assured with the translation of the Bible to the Yoruba language, which used the word Exu to translate demon." P. Adelumo D'pamu, *Exu: o inimigo invisível do homem*.

34. *As Ressignificações de Exu dentro da Umbanda*, Lenny Francis c. de Alvarenga.

of the devilish pact and the Sabbath of the witches, where the Devil reigned supreme, was imposed on the interpretation of the diverse rituals they found in Africa and America, reinforcing the association between the Devil and Esù and the recognition of the second as the Master of Magic, Magic being after Augustinian definition an art taught and empowered by devils in its inmost essence.

> What helped to accentuate in Brazil this element of wickedness, together with the popular dualism between good and evil, was the fact that Exu occupies a great place in magic. Some Exu or Legba are in Africa remarkable sorcerers and in Cuba, Exu is equally the Master of the Magic.[35]

EXUS AND POMBAGIRAS

From what we have seen above, we can understand how fundamental ideas about the orisha Esù passed to the descriptions of the Exus of Umbanda and Quimbanda, where they were married to ideas about the Devil and the witches. The identification, of course, begins with the use of the name *Exu* to identify the male spirits, and the name *Pombagira* to identify the female spirits, very likely derived from "Bonbonjira", used by the Bantu people in Angola, Congo and Moçambique for the same deity[36].

Some associations came easily. The rule of Esù over the ways and especially the crossroads linked it to the crossroads traditions of witchcraft going back to Hecate and Hermes. The power of Esù to open and close the ways was passed to Exus like Exu Tranca-Ruas (Exu Close the Streets). In Africa the offerings to Esù were left in the liminal places, like the entrances of houses, temples, and cities. In Umbanda, and even the shops where Umbanda material is sold, the place of honor of the Exus and Pombagiras are the doors

---

35. *Immigration et métamorphose d'um Dieu*, Roger Bastide.

36. *As Ressignificações de Exu dentro da Umbanda*, Lenny Francis c. de Alvarenga.

and entrances. The denomination of "People of the Street" given to Exus and Pombagiras possibly also came from the rule of Esù over the ways and the public places, like the markets. The association of the colors red and black, and with fire, also married perfectly the demonic imagery.

We can see very well the complex syncretism of Quimbanda in the following description given of the Exu Maioral. It combines the inheritance of the African orisha, the traditional ideas about the Devil, the influence of Kardecism, *and* a touch of Eliphas Levi. The influence of Eliphas Levi is clearly seen in Fontenelle's book.

> The Exu Maioral introduces himself as a being of high knowledge and wisdom in magic, and to him everything is possible, it is enough to believe that with certainty he will make your dream come true, no matter what it is.
>
> The Exu Maioral rules over a large phalanx of Exus and Pombagiras, giving them orders to execute many tasks and works here on earth. We use these magnificent powers to realize the strongest works of love binding, works of prosperity, spiritual cleansings, cure of sickness, release from vices and also to cut rivals and repel enemies.
>
> Many are fooled by saying that the Exus Maiorails are simply demons and backward spirits. Exu Maioral is the owner of a power and has many functions in the balance for the spiritual and material worlds.
>
> Exu is the movement of communication, he is what gives dynamis to the world with antagonic powers of movement and lethargy, because he was charged to give movement to the world and to make the communication between humans and the gods, the orishas. Exu Maioral is the Magical Agent, the ruling sorcerer who knows and dominates over all types of sorcery. Without him nothing can be done.

In all our experience in magic we always had as a foundation that Exu Maioral is a great Master in the teachings of sorcery that can never be received from the hands of a human being.[37]

We see here an inheritance of the descriptions given to the Sabbaths, where the Devil inquired of the deeds performed by the witches and her familiar spirits, giving to them rewards, punishments, and new orders, together with the Augustine view of the demons being the true teachers of magic. The "non-human" denomination given to the Exu Maioral in the quote above is more or less at odds with the current interpretation of the Exus and Pombagiras as being *eguns*, spirits of the dead. This new interpretation came under the influence of Kardecism, a doctrine that goes against almost every known spirit tradition when it rejects the idea of the existence of non-human spirits. The Exus and Pombagiras are usually seen as dead souls who led a degraded life on Earth, very often linked to abusive use of magic, a sinful sexual life, or great sufferings. Pombagiras are very often described as dead prostitutes, and the association between prostitutes and witchcraft, especially of the erotic kind, goes back a very long way, at least until the time of Rome. The tales about these spirits also often mention persons who became involved with magic and sorcery only *after* their death, when their spirits were adopted into a phalanx of Quimbanda. Pombagira, in some descriptions, is said to have given herself to or married with seven Exus, a strange idea for the African traditions which probably derived from the Iberian witchcraft, with its anonymous wives of the devils. These spirits would be inclined to perform any magical task if receiving proper payment, but when connected to a good Umbanda house they begin to restrict their performances to acceptable deeds. This ambiguity is very well attested in the Umbanda literature.

My personal experience divides the Exus and Pombagiras into two groups. One group is composed of non-human spirits whose main energies I define as "darkness" and "fire". By "darkness" I refer

---

37. This description is given on many internet sites, without mention of its source.

rather clumsily to a specific quality of energy as I perceive it. The other group I sense as being souls of the dead strongly charged with lunar energy. It is in the second group that I identify Maria Padilha of the Souls, my wife's patron and the influence behind this work.

THE MANY MARYS

The multiplying nature of Esù may be responsible for the ever growing number and descriptions of the Exus and Pombagiras. Some names are directly inherited from names and titles of the orisha Esù himself, like "Tiriri" (registered by Pierre Verger in Africa and Brazil, according to Reginaldo Prandi[38]); others seem to be descriptive of the qualities and characteristics of the spirit, like Exu Bat and Pombagira Rose Skull. In the retinue of Quimbanda, it seems that the only "true name" is the one belonging to Maria Padilha, a name that was already remarkable for being possibly the first name of a historical person to become a Goetic spirit in Europe since the Classical age.[39] Even real characters directly involved with Magic, as Agrippa, for instance, are sometimes mentioned in invocations,[40] but never *invoked* as spirits.

Nicholaj de Mattos Frisvold mentions nine different Maria Padilhas[41], divided through different spiritual kingdoms. It is

---

38. *Exu, de mesageiro a diabo - Sincretismo católico e demonização do orixá Exu*, Reginaldo Prandi.

39. That honor was after her also bestowed unto Enrique de Villena (1384-1434), who wrote one *Tratado de la fascinación o de aojamiento* (Treatise on the Evil Eye), and was considered after his death to be a necromancer. Upon his death his library was investigated by the Crown and the Church due to his supposed studies on Alchemy, Astrology, Philosophy, and Mathematics, and several books were burned. Later legends connect him with the Cave of Saint Cyprian in Salamanca, where he would have been a disciple to the magical arts taught by the Devil himself, acquiring there the knowledge that would have made him later very successful in the court. His name appears together with the name of Maria de Padilla in Spanish spells.

40. See for instance the *Sixth and Seventh Books of Moses*.

41. *Pomba Gira and the Quimbanda of Mbumba Nzila*, Nicholaj de Mattos Frisvold.

debatable if they represent different manifestations of the same spirit, like we see with the Virgin Mary, or different spirits sharing a special kind of kinship. Their names are:

> *Maria Padilha Queen of the Seven Crosses of the Cemetery*
> *Maria Padilha Queen of the Seven Crossroads*
> *Maria Padilha Queen of the Hells*
> *Maria Padilha Queen of the Souls*
> *Maria Padilha Queen of the Doors of the Cabaret*
> *Maria Padilha Queen of the Seven Razors*
> *Maria Padilha Queen of the Fig Tree*
> *Maria Padilha Queen of the Seven Catacombs*
> *Maria Padilha Queen of the Lyres*

The Sorcery of Maria Padilha

In this chapter we gather all the significant spells we could trace, where the name of Maria de Padilla or Maria Padilha appears. These spells range from the 17th to the 19th centuries.

Spell I comes from a process of the Inquisition against a gypsy witch who made her practice in the city of Madrid around 1624, and it is in fact a composition of three invocations made by the witch for the same client during a period of some weeks.[42] As was already noticed by scholars on the subject, the confessions of gypsy witches during the Spanish Inquisition never displayed any practice of conjuration that wasn't already known from non-gypsy sources.[43] Although Prosper Mérimée included in his novella *Carmen*, published in 1845, a scene where the gypsy protagonist performs a spell naming Maria Padella, who is called the *Bari Crallisa*, "the great gypsy queen", the truth of the matter is that the gypsies only came to Spain in the 15th century – a long time after the death of Maria de Padilla.

> I was hoping Carmen would have fled. She could have taken my horse and ridden away. But I found her there still. She did not choose that any one should say I had frightened her. While I had been away she had unfastened the hem of her gown and taken out the lead that weighted it; and now she was sitting before a table, looking into a bowl of water into which she had just thrown the lead she had melted. She was so busy with her spells that at first she didn't notice my return. Sometimes she would take out a bit of lead and turn it round every way with a melancholy look. Sometimes she would sing one of those magic songs, which invoke the help of Maria Padella, Don Pedro's

---

42. *La inquisicion y los gitanos*, de Maria Helena Sanchez Ortega.

43. *La inquisicion y los gitanos*, de Maria Helena Sanchez Ortega.

mistress, who is said to have been the *Bari Crallisa*–
the great gipsy queen.[44]

Spells II, III and IV came from gypsy witches prosecuted by
the Holy Office of Valencia in 1655.[45]

Spell V, also of gypsy origin, was published in 1882 by Antonio
Machado y Alvarez (1848-1893)[46], a Spanish writer, anthropologist,
and folklorist.

The magical secrets VI-IX came from the Portuguese edition
of the *Great Book of Saint Cyprian*, published at the end of the 19th
century.

I

Marta, Marta	Marta, Marta
La que en los infiernos estas,	Who in hell you are
Tres cabras tienes	You have three she-goats
y las ordeñas	and milk them
Y tres quesos harás,	And you will make three cheeses
El uno es para el diablo mayor,	One is for the great devil
El otro para su compañero,	The other for his companion
Y el otro para el diablo Cojuelo,	And the other for the Lame devil
O as como estas encadenada,	As you are chained
As venga este hombre atado y ligado,	So must this man come tied and bound
Y deje a Ana de Julio	And leave Ana de Julio
Con quien esta amancebado.	With whom he is cohabitating
As como esto yerbe,	As this boils
Yerbe el corazón de Blas,	Boils the heart of Blas
En el nombre de Satanas,	In the name of Satan
Y de Barrabás y del diablo Cojuelo	And of Barrabas and of the Lame devil
Y de su compañero	And of his companion
Y de la Jacarandina	And of the Jacarandina

---

44. *Carmen*, Prosper Merimee, translated by Lady Mary Loyd.

45. *La inquisicion y los gitanos*, de Maria Helena Sanchez Ortega.

46. *Biblioteca de las Tradiciones Populares Españolas*, Sevilla: Francisco
Álvarez y Cia.

Y de la Reina Sardina,	And of the Queen Sardina
Y de Doña María de Padilla	And of Lady Maria de Padilla
Y toda su cuadrilla,	And of all her cuadrilla
Y de Marta la que	And of Marta who
en los infiernos está.	in hell is
Marta, Marta,	Marta, Marta
La que en los infiernos estás	Who in hell you are
Acompañada de Satanás y Barrabás	Accompanied by Satan and Barrabas
Una cabra negra tienes	A black she-goat you have
Y tres escudillas de leche	And three bowls of milk you will
sacarás	take
Y tres quesos harás	And three cheeses you will make
El uno darás a Barrabás,	One you will give to Barrabas
El otro a Satanás,	The other to Satan
Y el otro a su compañero.	And the other to his companion

II

Por Barrabás, por Satanás y por	By Barrabas, by Satan and by
Lucifer	Lucifer
Por Doña Maria de Padilla	By Lady Maria de Padilla
Y toda su compania	And all her company
Que asi como hierve esta cazoleta	That as this small pan boils
Yerba el corazon de Fulano	Boils the heart of so-and-so
Que no pueda sosegar ni reposar	That he cannot calm and repose
Hasta que a Fulana venga a buscar.	Until he comes to fetch so-and-so

III

Yo te conjuro	I conjure you
Por Doña Maria de Padilla	By Lady Maria de Padilla
Con toda su cuadrilla	With all her cuadrilla
Por el Marqués de Villena	By the Marquis of Villena
Con toda su gente	With all his people
Por la mujer de Satanas	By the wife of Satan
Por la mujer de Barrabas	By the wife of Barrabas
Por la mujer de Belcebú	By the wife of Belcebu
Asi como estas tres estaban unidas	As these three were united
Y venian juntas con paz	And came together in peace
Venga el corazon de Fulano	Let the heart of so and so come
Atado, preso y enamorado.	Tied, bound and in love.

IV

Vecino y compadre	Neighbor and godfather
Gran Señor de la calle	Great Lord of the street
[aqui nombrará al galan]	[here you will name the man]
Solía venir a casa	Used to come to my house
Y ahora no viene	And now he doesn't come
Yo quiero que vengas	I want you to come
Si me lo has de traer	If you will bring him to me
Yo te conjuraré	I will conjure you
Con tres almas de mocicos enamorados	With three souls of lads in love
Con tres almas de desesperados	With three souls of desperate ones
Con el alma de Doña Maria de Padilla	With the soul of Lady Maria de Padilla
Y toda su cuadrilla	And all her cuadrilla
Todos os juntaréis	You will all gather
En compania iréis	And together you will go
En el corazón de Fulano entraréis	And into the heart of so-and-so you will enter
Y a mi casa lo traeréis	And to my house you will bring him
Muchas ansias le daréis	You will give him many anguishes
Que no le dejéis reposar	That do not let him rest
Hasta que me venga a buscar	Until he comes to fetch me
Dándome lo que tuviere	Giving to me what he has
Y diciéndome lo que supiere	And saying to me what he knows

V

Conjuro para conquistar a una mujer — *Conjuration to conquer a woman*

Estrella, estrella	Star, star,
más alta y más bella	the highest and most beautiful
tres rayos tienes	three rays you have
y tres rayos tendrás	and three rays you will have
uno, el demonio mayor[47]	one, the great demon

---

47. It is tempting to see in the recurrent expression "demonio mayor" the origin of the Portuguese denomination Maioral.

el segundo y el tercero	the second and the third
que es el lamo (sic) más pajuelo[48]	who is the lord most horned
más pronto y más ligero	more ready and more fast
Diablos, venid	Devils, come
os conjuro a todos juntos	I conjure you all together
que no puedo disparar ni sosegar	because I cannot run neither rest
que cuando me véis en apuro	when you see me in trouble
me librará	you will free me
de todo lo que te pido	everything I ask you
me lo otorgará	you will grant to me
esta oración te digo	this orison I say to you
para que pueda alcanzar	So you I can gain
mujeres por muy bravas que las veas	Women no matter how brave they would be
Esta oración que echo	This orison I made
para que te quedes mansa	To make you tame,
te conjuro con María Padilla	I conjure with María Padilla
y con toda su cuadrilla	and all her cuadrilla
que lo que pido me lo otorgará	that what I ask you will grant to me
y por muy brava que esté	And no matter how brave you are
se me amansará	You will be tamed to me

VI

*Another magic of the black cat, and the way
of generating a little devil with the eyes of the cat*

Kill a black cat, and after it is dead, take his eyes and put them inside the egg of a black hen, but, taking note that each eye must be separated inside each egg. After this operation is done, put it into a pile of horse manure, and it is necessary that the manure is very warm to generate there the little devil.

Saint Cyprian says that you must go every day to the said pile of manure, that during one month, the time the little devil takes to be born.

---

48. The original meaning being uncertain, and the word "pajuelo" not being a recognized word, this is a tentative translation where I consider that "lamo", indicates "amo", meaning "lord" or "master".

WORDS THAT MUST BE SAID BY THE
PILE OF MANURE WHERE THE LITTLE DEVIL IS

Oh great Lucifer, I deliver unto you these two eyes of a black cat, so you, my great friend Lucifer, be favorable in this appellation that I do at your feet. My great minister and friend Satanaz and Barabbas, I deliver unto you the black magic so you put on it all your power, virtue and astuteness that were given to you by Jesus Christ; because I deliver to you these two eyes of a black cat, so from them a devil will born to be my companion eternally. My black magic, I deliver you to Maria Padilha and all her family and to all the devils in hell, lames, weak-sighted, crippled and to all that is infernal, so from this two devils are born to give me money, because I want money by the power of Lucifer, my friend and companion from now on.

Do all this that we just indicated, and at the end of one month, a day less or a day more, two little devils will be born to you, with the figure of a small lizard. As soon as the little devil is born, put it into a small tube of ivory or boxwood and give to him to eat iron or ground steel...

When you be the owner of the two little devils you can do whatever pleases you; for instance: do you want money? Just open the tube and say: I want money here now, and it immediately appears to you, with only one condition that you cannot give alms to the poor and neither pay for Masses to be said, because it is money given by the demon.

Readers: It is not possible to describe in this 2ª part of the *Great Book of Saint Cyprian* or *Treasure of the Sorcerer*, all that happened to this Saint, because to do it we would need to make a great volume, that would not be possible to be bought by all classes of people, as a consequence of the high price it would cost.

We limit ourselves, then, to teach you all the sorceries Saint Cyprian used during his life as a sorcerer, and you, readers, will well understand what a creature can achieve having the wonderful power of the magical art.

VII

*Magic or sorcery to be made with two
dolls to cause harm to any person*

Observe with attention what we will teach, to be sure this magic is well done.

Take two dolls; one of them signifies the creature to whom you are going to do the spell, and the other signifies the one who is going to cast the spell.

After the said dolls are ready, you must unite one to the other, in a way that they are tightly embraced. After all that is done tie both with a sewing thread around the neck like if you are strangling them, and after this operation is done fix five nails in them, at the indicated parts:

1ª – In the head, piercing through one and the other.
2ª – In the chest, in the same way.
3ª – In the belly, piercing from one side to the other.
4ª – In the legs, piercing from one side to the other.
5ª – In the feet, in a way that drills from one side to the other.

In this way that creature will suffer the same pains as if the nails were fixed in his own body.

There is also one more condition, that is, that the said nails be fixed with the saying of the following invocations in the different places where they are fixed:

1° nail – So and so, I, so and so, nail you, bind and pierce your body, as I pierce, tie and nail your figure.

2° nail – So and so, I, so and so, I swear under the power of Lucifer and Satanaz, that from now to the future you will not have even one hour of health.

3° nail – So and so, I, so and so, swear under the power of the ill-wishing magic, that from today to the future you will not have one hour of peace.

4° nail - So and so, I, so and so, swear under the power of Maria Padilha, that from today to the future you will be possessed by all spells.

5° nail - So and so, I, so and so, bind and tie you from the feet to the head by the power of the sorcerous magic.

This way the ensorcelled creature never more will have one hour of health.

Readers, do not be scared with this, because God, as He gave to men power and wisdom to make spells, he also gave medicine to fight against them, as it is explained in the first part of this work, which teaches how to unmake all kinds of sorcery - which is the life of Saint Cyprian, when he was Saint, and this is why we recommend to every Christian to have this book.

DECLARATION

In order that you do not doubt what you just read, it will be good to give you an explanation, and it is the following:

It needs to be two dolls united one to the other, the one who will be ensorcelled and one who will ensorcell; meaning, the one who ensorcells is embraced to the ensorcelled wanting to kill him or pierce him with the nails.

VIII

Sorcery to be done with five nails
taken from the coffin of a dead man,
that means, when it is already taken from the grave

Enter a cemetery and bring from there five nails from the coffin of a dead man, but always with the thought fixed on the sorcery you are going to do.

After that draw over a wooden board a sign of Solomon where you must have a sign from the person you are going to ensorcell; this sign must be nailed to the sign of Solomon.

THE WAY YOU WILL FIX THE NAILS
AND THE WORDS YOU MUST SAY
WHEN FIXING THEM

1° nail – (say the name of the person you are ensorcelling). So and so, I beseech you, in the name of Satanaz, Barabbas and Caifaz, so you be bound to me, as Lucifer is bound in the deep of the hell.

2° nail – So and so, I bind and tie you inside this sign of Solomon; as the Cross of Jesus Christ inside this sign was buried and the blood of Jesus on it was spilled, so I (so and so), cite and notify so you will not fail me on this, by the spilled blood of Jesus Christ.

3° nail – So and so, I bind you to me, eternally, as Satanaz is bound in hell.

4° nail – So and so, I so and so bind you and tie you inside this sign of Solomon, so you do not have peace or rest unless you are in my company, this by the power of Satanaz and of Maria Padilha and all her family.

5° nail – So and so, only when God stops being God and the deceased to whom these nails served speak, is when you will leave me.

We declare that when the last word is said you must give a great strike to the nail.

At the end of all of this keep the wooden board and when you want to undo the sorcery burn it.

IX

*Sorcery made with a bat
to make someone love*

Let's suppose that a girlfriend wants to marry with her boyfriend with great brevity. Do it as follows:

Take a bat and pass through its eyes a needle with a sewing thread.

After this operation the needle and the sewing thread acquire a great force of sorcery.

WAY TO ENSORCELL

Take an object of the person you want to ensorcell and make five cross shaped knots, saying the following words:

So and so, I ensorcell you by the power of Maria Padilha and all her family so you do not see neither the sun neither the moon as long as you do not marry me, that by the power of the sorcerous magic of the middle age.

After all that is executed, as it is written, the ensorcelled person does not have one hour of peace until he marries.

If perhaps you do not want to marry the ensorcelled person anymore, you must burn the object on which the sorcery was made.

X

Remedy against humpbacks

To avoid your business going wrong when in the morning you meet some humpback, Saint Cyprian says to do as follows:

Dolphin, hunchback, who crooks towards, vac, vac, diligent, and leave me in peace. Dolphin, dolphin, do not chase me: there goes one figa, do not look back.

With this make a figa with the left hand and extend the right arm with the hand open, making mention of catching a butterfly.

Then you keep walking with the closed hand until you find one of these fellows:

Another humpback
One municipal soldier

One white horse
One lame
One one-handed person
One black cat
One dog, idem
One albino man

As soon as you find one of these fellows, open the hand saying in a continuous act:

Go in the name of Maria Padilha and all her family, to where you cannot bother neither a rich or a poor man, and neither anyone covered by the sky.

This conjuration is infallible; we have used it on many occasions and we always avoid crossing by hunchbacks, who are fatidic to who see them, although they are not guilty of that.

IMPORTANT PREVENTION

To have this recipe producing a healthy effect it is necessary to not have hate toward the humpback, otherwise, everything will go wrong for the person.

THE INVOCATION OF MARIA PADILHA

The *ponto cantados* ("chanted points"), sung invocations where the old Iberian spells became mixed with the ceremonial African music, are one of the main characteristics of the Umbanda and Quimbanda ceremonies. We selected some *pontos cantados* where we can see how the image and importance of Maria Padilha has evolved. In some *pontos cantados* she took the position of the previously unnamed wives of Lucifer and Satanaz; she is called "goddess of sorcery" and "the owner of the black magic". All this shows the popular recognition of the process of apotheosis through which the spirit of the dead queen has being ascending.

During our research we found some references to prophecies where it is said that Maria Padilha will not manifest in the same way anymore – that she will rise to the level of the orishas, or equivalent things. That would not be so out of context, as there exist some interpretations where the orishas are believed to have been kings and queens of the first times, who became divinized – just like Osiris and Isis were said to have been. One of these prophecies goes like this:

> There is a prophecy which says that in the year 2000 Maria Padilha, the Queen of the queens, will step over the Orishas. The Orishas will revere her because her mission is to convert the man she loves (Lucifer, angel of darkness). They will enter the house of God both dressed in white. She will sit by the side of Jesus Christ and him at the feet of Christ. Maria Padilha will save 7000 souls and will deliver to the flames of hell 7000 more souls.[49]

---

49. http://br.answers.yahoo.com/question/index?qid=20070427145752AAfQyd6

I

Mas ela é a Maria Padilha, / But she is the Maria Padilha
Mulher da máfia, / Woman of the mafia,
é mulher de Lucifer / woman of Lucifer
Oi, ela gira nas / Hey, she spins around in the
noites escuras / dark nights
O seu feitiço tá na / Her spell is at the
ponta do seu garfo / tip of her fork
Tá de baixo do seu pé / Is under her foot
Me chaman de leviana, / They call me frivolous
E até mesmo mulher de cabaré / Even a woman of the cabaret
Mas a língua do povo / But the tongue of the people does
não tem osso / not have bone
Então deixa esse povo falar / Then let the people talk
Mas a língua do povo / But the tongue of the people does
não tem osso / not have bone
Então deixa esse povo falar / Then let the people talk

II

Maria balança a saia / Maria swings the skirt
Mas não deixa a saia cair / But she does not let the skirt fall
Se seu pai é feiticeiro / If her father is a sorcerer
sua mãe catimbozeira / Her mother is *catimbozeira*[50]
chegou Maria Padilha / Maria Padilha arrived
dona da magia negra... / The owner of the black magic...

Ia passando na encruza / I was passing by the crossroad
Quando avistei uma armadilha / When I saw a trap
Eu sou Pombagira / I am Pombagira
Eu sou Maria Padilha / I am Maria Padilha

Maria Padilha é a mulher de / Maria Padilha is the wife of
Satanaz / Satanaz
Eu quero ver ela, no inferno ela é / I want to see her, in hell she is
a mulher que pode mais / the woman who can do more

Maria Padilha por que não casou / Maria Padilha why did you not marry
foi uma gota serena que o devil / It was a sorrow the devil
mandou... / sent...

---

50. From Catimbó, a mágico-religious system from the Northeast Brazil, originating in the 17th century after the syncretism of Native American rituals and European magical practices.

Vou escrever com seu sangue na areia	I will write with your blood in the sand
mas que saudade da minha aldeia	Oh, how I miss my village
o pombo preto bateu asa e voou	The black pigeon flapped its wings and flew
Maria Padilha vai embora mas deixou o seu amor...	Maria Padilha goes away but left her love...
Ela é Padilha ela é dama mulher	She is the Padilha she is a lady woman
Ela deu seu sangue em vida ao rei Lúcifer	She gave her blood during her life to the king Lucifer
O rei Lúcifer mandou lhe chamar	The king Lucifer ordered her to be called
Coroada no inferno ela é rainha de lá	Crowned in hell she is the queen there
Tem mulher de chifre tem mulher de rabo	There are woman with horns, there are woman with tails
Ela é Maria Padilha, a mulher do diabo...	She is Maria Padilha, the wife of the devil...
Eu ia andando devagar	I was walking slowly
Eu ia andando bem ligeiro	I was walking fast
Chamei a Padilha dos 7 cruzeiros	I called the Padilha of the 7 Cruzeiros
Eu vi raiar o sol	I saw the sun rise
Eu vi sumir a lua	I saw the moon disappear
Chamei a Padilha no meio da rua	I called the Padilha in the middle of the street

III

Maria Padilha é uma feiticeira	Maria Padilha is a sorcerer
mais n gosta de falar	but she does not like to talk
Maria Padilha é um a feiticeira	Maria Padilha is a sorcerer
mais n gosta de falar	But she does not like to talk
O feitiço q ela faz, ela faz é pra matar	The sorcery she does, is to kill
O feitiço q ela faz, ela faz é pra matar	The sorcery she does, is to kill

IV

Maria Padilha das Almas	Maria Padilha of the Souls
Padilha soberana das almas	Padilha sovereign of the souls
Rainha do cemitério e também do	Queen of the cemetery and also

candomblé.	Of the *candomblé*
Suprema é mulher de negro	Supreme is the woman in black
Alegria do terreiro	The joy of the *terreiro*
Seu feitiço tem axé.	Her sorcery has *ashè*
Mas ela é,	But she is
ela é,ela é	She is, she is
A rainha da calunga	The queen of the *calunga*
A mulher de Lúcifer	The wife of Lucifer
Quem viu o sol se esconder	Who saw the sun hide
Quem viu a lua brilhar	Who saw the moon shine
Quem viu o espinho da rosa	Who saw the thorn of the rose
Também vai ver	Will also see
Maria Padilha chegar	Maria Padilha arrive
Os seus olhos são verdes	Her eyes are green
Sua cor é mulata	Her color is brown
Seus cabelos são negros	Her hair is black
E a sandália é de prata	And the sandal is made of silver
Numa mão tem perfume	In one hand she has perfume
Na outra tem a flor	In the other a flower
Pra Umbanda querida	To the beloved Umbanda
Maria Padilha traz paz	Maria Padilha brings peace
E traz amor.	And brings love
Maria Padilha Feiticeira	Maria Padilha Sorcerer
Feiticeira	Sorcerer
Maria Padilha da calunga	Maria Padilha of the *calunga*
O seu feitiço não é de brincadeira	Her sorcery is not a plaything
Maria Padilha da calunga	Maria Padilha of the *calunga*
Ela trabalha sem parar	She works around the clock
Se a sua catatumba tem mistérios	If her catacomb has mysteries
Mas ela é Maria Padilha do cemitério	But she is Maria Padilha of the cemetery
Mas ela é loira	But she is blond
Olhos azuis	Blue eyed
Maria Padilha mensageira de Omulu	Maria Padilha a messenger of Omulu
Deu meio-dia	The noon came
Deu meia-noite	Midnight came
Maria Pdilha mensageira de	Maria Padilha messenger of

Omulu	Omulu
Mas ela vem girando na linha das almas	But she comes spinning around in the line of the souls
É a Maria Padilha	She is Maria Padilha
Mas ela vem girando na linha das almas	But she comes spinning around in the line of the souls
É a Maria Padilha	She is the Maria Padilha
É só quando eu toco tambor	It is only when I play the drum
É só quando eu toco pra ela	It is only when I play for her
O seu olhar é sereno	Her glance is serene
O seu olhar me fascina	Her glance fascinates me
Maria Padilha é uma deusa uma santa?	Maria Padilha, is she a goddess or a saint?
É uma deusa uma santa?	Is she a goddess or a saint?
Ela é o que?	What is she?
Ela é o devil!	She is the devil!

V

Vocês tão vendo aquela bruxa parada	Do you see that witch still
aquela bruxa sentada	That witch sitting
aquela bruxa em pé	That witch standing
seu nome é Maria Padilha	Her name is Maria Padilha
a deusa da feitiçaria	The goddess of sorcery

VI

Maria Padilha das Almas	Maria Padilha of the Souls
Quando Passar na porta do Cemitério moço	When you pass by the door of the cemetery, man
toma cuidado não olha pra atrás	Take care to not look back
Mas é que lá	Because there
tem uma moça vestida de branco moço	There is a lady dressed in white
ela é Maria Maria	She is Maria, Maria
Ela é Maria, Maria	She is Maria, Maria
Ela é Maria, Maria	She is Maria, Maria
Ela é Maria, Maria	She is Maria, Maria
Maria Padilha das Almas	Maria Padilha of the Souls
Ela é Maria, Maria	She is Maria, Maria

Ponto Riscado

The *pontos riscados* ("drawn points") are talismanic images used to invoke spirits in Umbanda and Quimbanda. They usually are composed, in the case of Exus and Pombagiras, of a circle containing arrows, forks, crosses, stars, skulls, and other related symbols. Often a spirit presents more than one *ponto riscado*, depending on what will be asked of her. The most probable origin of the *pontos riscados* is in the circles and Solomonic symbols of European magic, used in simplified ways by Portuguese witches. As an example, we see in an Inquisition process of 1673 the following narrative:

> She used to make a sign of Solomon, in which she the accused entered, and two chairs, by the side of the said sign of Solomon, and then she said certain words, and soon two shadows appeared, one of man and the other of woman, whom she said was Maria Padilha, with whom she spoke from the sign of Solomon, saying to her: *Maria de Padilha, ask your lover Erasmo, by the torments he suffered for you, to do what I ask of you.* And then she asked what she wanted. And soon the figure of Maria Padilha asked the other shadow which she said was Erasmo, to do what she asked. And the other shadow called, without being understandable to whom, and soon an amount of pigs came, and between them a lame one, to whom the said shadow ordered what was asked to be done. And the accused kept doing the practice to the said shadows during one hour, because if she did not do so they would beat her a lot.[51]

The above account is very interesting, because it brings into view again the ideas of the legions or phalanxes of demons

---

51. *Maria Padilha e toda a sua quadrilha*, Marlyse Meyer.

(the many pigs led by the lame one) associated with the souls of the dead, and of the souls of the dead assuming commanding positions in the afterlife. Also important is the position of the witch as being somehow under an obligation to her patron spirits – all very close concepts to the Quimbanda.

The next image shows the most common *ponto riscado* of Maria Padilha. The devil fork with round points is usually associated with the Pombagiras, and the straight ones with the Exus, but I found references that the round ones could also indicate the People of Cemetery and the straight the People of the Street, basic divisions of the Quimbanda spirits. However, the general observations follow more the first explanation.

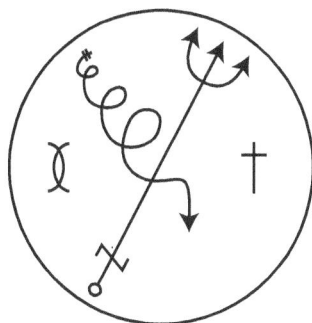

The idea and the inspiration of this small work we present to the reader came from one direct contact I had with my wife's patron, Maria Padilha of the Souls. As the work suggested by the spirit progressed, Maria Padilha of the Souls gave me several ideas and inspirations concerning general issues of my life which had astounding positive results. Following coincidences, I came to the invocation I had already known for years from Crowley's major opus *The Vision and the Voice*, and found it remarkably apt to a work with Pombagira (see the following). Sometime after that, in another direct contact, Maria Padilha of the Souls gave to me the following *ponto riscado*:

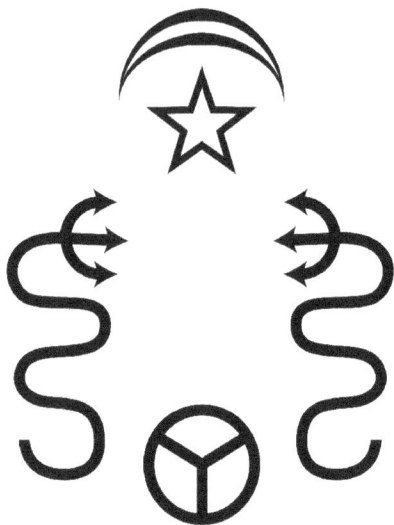

In the following weeks I followed a thread of insights and coincidences inspired by the *ponto riscado*. The *ponto riscado* is not traditional in the sense that it is not contained in a circle. The preeminence of the Moon is in agreement with my perception of the lunar energies of these kind of entities, and I understood the star as making reference to the proper moments to work the indicated sorceries: the conjunctions of Moon with Mercury, Venus, Mars, Jupiter, and Saturn.

The circle with its triple division insinuates many interpretations. First, the triple crossroad, the crossroad favored by the Pombagiras. It can indicate a place of offering or the offering itself, as the triple division is linked to the three different kinds of *ashè*, or magical energy of the Universe which is the main element in some of the African traditions. The concept of *ashè* has close connotations with the divine and magical energies we find in European magic. An apt description is enough to bring the point to mind:

[...] the most precious content of a terreiro is the ashè. It is the force which assures the dynamic existence, which allows the happening and the future. Without ashè, the existence would be paralyzed, devoid of every possibility of realization. It is the principle which makes possible the vital process. As every force, the ashè is transmissible; it is conducted by material and symbolic means and is accumulable. It is a force that can only be transmitted by introjection or by contact. It can be transmitted to objects or to human beings [...] [It is] an invisible force, the magical-sacred force of every divinity, of every animated being, of everything. But this force does not appear spontaneously; it must be transmitted. Every object, being or place is only consecrated through the acquisition of ashè. So it is understood that the terreiro, with all its material contents and its initiates, must receive ashè, accumulate it, keep it and develop it.[52]

The *ashè* is contained in mineral, vegetal, and animal elements, and is classified in three types: red, white, and black. So, a complete general offering would include nine items, made of three elements of each type of *ashè*. In the table below we offer some examples:[53]

	RED	WHITE	BLACK
MINERAL	Copper	Silver	Coal, Iron
VEGETAL	Honey	Alcohol	Dark juice of some vegetables
ANIMAL	Menstrual blood, human blood, animal blood	Semen	Ashes of animals

---

52. *Os Nago e a Morte*, Juana Elbein dos Santos.
53. *Os Nago e a Morte*, Juana Elbein dos Santos.

The *ashè* is the currency between the realms, and from this we can see the inevitable connection with Esù. The offerings made in Quimbanda descend directly from the complex system of African offerings.

All these things I found out after Maria de Padilha of the Souls suggested this work, and they are in harmony with some information she provided before about a special kind of work to be performed with my wife, which involved an offering in a golden cup of menstrual blood, semen, and some herbs of which she would tell her later. All these of course bring us to the province of Crowley's tantric-derived teachings, and I see a similarity between the two fork-serpents in the *ponto riscado* and the Lion and Eagle figures in the Atus VI and XIV of the Thoth Tarot, pouring the sexual fluids into the cauldron. The two fork-serpents seem to indicate an offering made by two persons, and also bring to my mind the Caduceus of Hermes. Menstrual blood and semen are substances often found in Portuguese folk magic.[54]

The golden cup, shown to me in a vision by Maria de Padilha of the Souls, also brings to mind Thelemic connections with the Scarlet Woman and Babalon, concepts linked to practices of sexual magic dealing with blood and semen. It connects to the mentioned song from *The Vision and the Voice*, revealed during Crowley's visions of the Aethyr of Babalon.

The *Conjuration to conquer a woman* we saw before also provided me with other interpretations for the revealed *ponto riscado*. It led me to associate the three lines dividing the circle with the tripartite division of the world by the Chiefs of the *Grimorium Verum*, adopted in some descriptions of the Quimbanda hierarchy, as we saw. The position of the circle under the heavens, symbolized by the Moon and the Star, is in agreement with all the classical denominations for the *loci daemonorum* in the sub-lunar world.

The two fork-serpents may also indicate not just two participants in an offering ceremony, but a couple of spirits attending to it. We must remember that Maria de Padilha is recurrently

---

54. *Inferno Atlântico, Demonologia e Colonização nos Séculos XVI-XVIII,* Laura de Mello e Souza.

associated with major male demons, an association which seems to be old, as we saw in the Inquisition process of 1673.

One element in the song of Babalon especially called my attention, the "seven-stringed instrument" named "barbiton". It is "an ancient stringed instrument known from Greek and Roman classics related to the lyre".[55] The relation to the lyre inevitably reminded me of one of the spiritual divisions of Quimbanda, the Kingdom of the Lyre. According to Frisvold, the main exponent of the craft, the Kingdom of the Lyre "is presided over by Maria Padilha Rainha of the Seven Hells" and "it is headed by Exu Lucifer".[56] Still according to Frisvold:

> The Queen of the Kingdom of the Lyre is seen by many as the most pure and ideal manifestations of Pomba Gira. This Queen is the wife of Exu Seven Lyres and some say Seven Lilies – better known as Exu Lucifer, brother of Exu Mor, also known as Nine Lights. Interestingly, the lyre can mean three things: it can be the lyre, it can be the lily and it can also be the little district Lira close to Baganda in Angola. This is her crossroad, the lyre being a symbol for her seductiveness and affinity with dance and the arts. The lily is clearly a reference to her potency for macumba and lastly, the African district that manifests three legs of her preferred crossroad, where three worlds meet and make nine kingdoms.[57]

Although I developed the idea that the star in the *ponto riscado* indicates the five planets, my initial intuition was that Moon and Venus, the feminine astrological representatives, were being represented. Besides considerations linked to witchcraft traditions where Lunar

55. http://en.wikipedia.org/wiki/Barbiton

56. *Pomba Gira and the Quimbanda of Mbumba Nzila*, Nicholaj de Mattos Frisvold.

57. *Pomba Gira and the Quimbanda of Mbumba Nzila*, Nicholaj de Mattos Frisvold.

goddesses are married to Lucifer (the Morning Star), there are several correspondences to be drawn from the Kabbalah of the Thoth Tarot of Crowley – if we follow the thread of inspirations and insights Maria Padilha of the Souls seems to be weaving for this work.

First, we see that the Moon and Venus in the Kabbalah of the Thoth Tarot are directly connected in a *crossroad*: they are represented by the Atus II and III, the Priestess and the Empress, which in turn are marked by the Hebrew letters Gimel and Daleth (see the crossroad made by their Paths in the Tree of Life).

Second, the *ponto riscado* visually recalls very closely the design of the Atu named "The Moon"; although in the Crowley deck it is attributed to the sign Pisces. But the design is clear: the Moon above, the way surrounded by two chthonic animals (the fork-serpents substituting for the dogs or wolves). According to Crowley, the Priestess Atu represents "the most purest exalted conception of the Moon", and the Moon in the Pisces Atu is "at the other end of the scale".[58]

> The Moon, partaking as she does of the highest and the lowest, and filling all the space between, is the most universal of the Planets. In her higher aspect, she occupies the place of the Link between the human and divine, as shown in Atu II. In this Trump, her lowest avatar, she joins the earthy sphere of Netzach with Malkuth, the culmination in matter of all superior forms. This is the waning moon, the moon of witchcraft and abominable deeds. She is the poisoned darkness which is the condition of the rebirth of light. This path is guarded by Tabu. She is uncleanliness and sorcery. Upon the hills are the black towers of nameless mystery, of horror and of fear. All prejudice, all superstition, dead tradition and ancestral loathing, all combine to darken her face before the eyes of men.[59]

58. *The Book of Thoth*, Aleister Crowley.
59. *The Book of Thoth*, Aleister Crowley.

All that coincides perfectly with the multiple possibilities open in the work with Maria Padilha. She can be an initiatrix of hidden and profound mysteries, but she is also linked to the basest forms of Magic.

As often happens when dealing with Spirit Masters, the research we are committed to ends in unexpected ways, but when we come to this, it seems to make perfect sense.

Quimbanda suffers from two great hindrances: its unsuccessful attempts at conforming to Christianity first, and then to Kardec doctrines. The spirits of Quimbanda cannot be properly understood according to these mistaken descriptions of the spiritual reality, and trying to do so has just limited the scope of the possible work.

The path tread during the research and writing of this work seems to indicate a willingness of these spirits to come closer to a more harmonic form of interpretation about their natures and work. The approximation with Thelema, a philosophical-magical system to which I do not profess a religious acceptance, but from which I inherited key concepts of my view of life, seems to be an inevitable occurrence, a marriage of fate.

Quimbanda has been described as being originally a magical weapon used by the oppressed people: the slaves and the exiled, the pagans and the heretics who were forced to live in Brazil, persecuted by State and Church. As Quimbanda forces its way now to freedom from the ideology of the oppressor, it will become once again a legion against the tyranny of the current status quo.

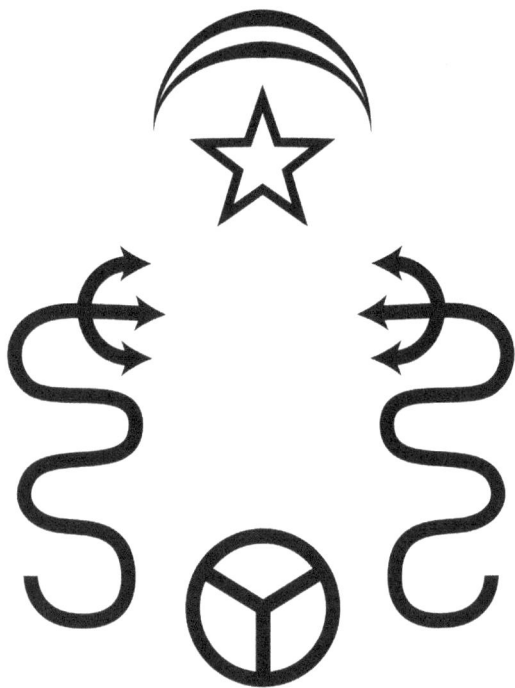

Omari tessala marax
I am the harlot that shaketh Death

tessala dodi phornepax
This shaking giveth the Peace of Satiated Lust

amri radara poliax
Immortality jetteth from my skull

armana piliu
And music from my vulva

amri radara piliu son
Immortality jetteth from my vulva also

mari narya barbiton
For my Whoredom is a sweet scent like a seven-stringed instrument

madara anaphax sarpedon
Played unto God the Invisible, the all-ruler

andala hriliu
That goeth along giving the shrill scream of orgasm

Every man that hath seen me forgetteth me never, and I appear oftentimes in the coals of the fire, and upon the smooth white skin of woman, and in the constancy of the waterfall, and in the emptiness of deserts and marshes, and upon great cliffs that look seaward; and in many strange places, where men seek me not. And many thousand times he beholdeth me not. And at last I smite myself into him as a vision smiteth into a stone, and whom I call must follow.

Maria de Padilla, Maria Padilha: a résumé

1334 Birth of Maria de Padilla, daughter of Juan Garcia de Padilla and Maria Gonzáles de Hinestrosa. Her family is part of the local nobility and originally from the village of Padilla de Abajo.

1352 Maria de Padilla meets the king Pedro I, probably through her maternal uncle, who was close to the king.

1353 Pedro I marries Blanche de Bourbon, but leaves her three days after the wedding to return to Maria de Padilla. Some of the alleged reasons were a flirtation between Blanche and his half-brother Fadrique and the nonpayment of the dowry.

Maria de Padilla founds the Royal Monastery of Saint Claire of Astudillo, where she plans to live.

Birth of Beatriz, first daughter of Pedro I and Maria de Padilla.

1354 Birth of Constanza de Borgona, second daughter of Pedro I and Maria de Padilla.

1355 Birth of Isabel de Castilla, third daughter of Pedro I and Maria de Padilla.

1359 Birth of Alfonso de Castilla, son of Pedro I and Maria de Padilla.

1361 Maria de Padilla dies and is buried in the Royal Monastery of Saint Claire of Astudillo, but is later transferred to the Cathedral of Seville.

1362 Death of Alfonso de Castilla, son of Pedro I and Maria de Padilla.

1369 Death of Beatriz, first daughter of Pedro I and Maria de Padilla.

Death of Pedro I de Castilla.

1392 Death of Isabel de Castilla, third daughter of Pedro I and Maria de Padilla.

1394 Death of Constanza de Borgona, second daughter of Pedro I and Maria de Padilla.

1579 Maria de Padilla's remains are transferred to the new Royal Chapel inside the Cathedral of Seville.

1624 Maria de Padilla's name appears in a spell in the tribunal of the Holy Office in Madrid.

1841 The debut of the opera in three acts *Maria Padilla*, with music by Gaetano Donizetti (1797-1848) and libretto by Gaetano Rossi (1774-1855).

1845 Prosper Mérimée (1803-1870), French dramatist, historian and archaeologist, publishes his novella *Carmen*, where Maria Padella [sic] is mentioned in a spell.

Oniric phantasy by the French artist Jean Paul Gervais (1859-1936), about María de Padilla, presenting herself naked to the King Pedro.

POST SCRIPTUM

After finishing my part of this work, I continued to use the *ponto riscado* in my practices, having it printed and making offerings of red candles and white *ashè*. During one of these practices, I was moved to read again *The Cry of the 2nd Aethyr Which is called ARN*[60] and could see many more connections. There is the marriage of Woman and Devil in "the legend of Eve and the Serpent", and there also is to be found the Three Chiefs of Hell, under the names of Lucifer, Belial, and Satan – which I sensed could be used as the head of a fiery-solar Quimbanda hierarchy, which of course would adapt very well with all the trinities in Thelema.

Also the Moon figures prominently, and sacrifices and offerings of blood are present.

I also saw how some features of the foundational text of Thelema, *The Book of the Law*, brings it close to Quimbanda, a cult where the sacrifice of cattle, little and big, and many other things, figure prominently.

I was moved to call the Aethyr, and finished it accepting the offer of a Pact.

---

60. *The Vision and the Voice*, Aleister Crowley.

SECOND PART

THE
SKYDANCER

by
VERÓNICA RIVAS

INTRODUCTION

My first contact with Maria Padilha, Queen of the Souls, was something that had a great impact on me. I knew nothing about Kimbanda, as my focus and study were on Eastern traditions, but having established contact with Kimbanda, I became interested in the ability of human beings to invoke spirit, which goes back to the most ancient of times that humankind can remember.

After a passage of time spent away from Kimbanda, during which I established closer contact with the practices of Vajrayana Buddhism, the presence of Maria Padilha returned to me, but in a different way. I began to feel that the perception we have of spirits depends mainly on two aspects: the cultural and social environment in which we live and why we are invoking the spirit. I started to note the similarities between the kingdom of Exu and, more specifically, the figure of the pombagira, with other spirits belonging to the Hindu or Tibetan traditions.

In the course of my personal contacts with Maria Padilha – by which I mean without pre-established rituals or initiations – I began to feel that she is a spirit who is beyond what it largely thought about her, and that she, as a great sorceress who has reached high levels of accomplishments and knowledge, presents herself as a great teacher of high magic and a gatekeeper of the secret knowledge.

Magic can be understood as a practice through which it is possible to have an effect on certain factors or events in our existence as well as in the existence of other beings. Magical practices present themselves as a process, one that implies learning, apprehension, and revealing. From a tantric point of view, the magical process opens the gates to fulfillment and transcendence – magic is not something acquired through learning, but something that we learn in order to wake up to a new perception of reality, as an inherent quality. Absolutely everything that surrounds us is basically energy that is moving and manifesting itself in many different ways. The profound understanding of the way energy informs all things, the way that it interacts with us and our self in the world, is what the practice of magic is about.

However, our connection with magic does not appear to us as something natural. For most people, it is a kind of recourse that emerges when we need something – from a sense of loss, from the feeling that we are looking for something. In most cases, it emerges from the desperation to obtain the favor of a "spiritual being" or an entity who can give us the job that we desire, or to bring back the person we love. If we take a look at the liturgies, the Christian prayers from which our society was molded, we see examples of this. We basically perceive someone unsatisfied, someone who feels that they are incapable of something, and in order to obtain what he/she wants, tries to pact with a spiritual entity. Notwithstanding, the oriental liturgies, and the Tibetan ones in particular, sound different: the person who is trying to communicate with the deity or spirit is not asking for his or her mercy or to intercede for him or her, but to conquer or develop certain qualities in order to direct his or her energy to a specific goal.

A great system of magical practices is one that formed when the African beliefs took shape in Brazil – we are referring here to Kimbanda. We can define it rapidly as a group of ritualistic practices, shamanic in their essence, but strongly influenced by many other thoughts like Christianity and native belief, but mostly by the Kardecist point of view.

To the Kardecist, when an Exu spirit arrives, it is treated as a low astral being who should be "indoctrinated", because for them, the spirits are in a process of lineal evolution for which they need human intervention in order to pass from a low state to a superior one. This is the procedure with all kinds of spirits who share certain qualities with the Exus. They are treated as spirits from darkness, low-grade, and with such a negative karma that they do not have any kind of wisdom to pass onto us. From my point of view, these perspectives contribute to creating an image of Exus and pombagiras as beings who only have power to act in material matters or sexual issues.

In many cases, they are seen as revengeful beings, attached to matter and through whom the oppressed sectors of the society reflect and manifest their frustrations. From this perspective, the duty of these spirits as guardians of instructions, as holders of the key of knowledge and magical arts, is left aside.

Somehow, I always had the tendency to perceive the Exu entity with oriental eyes. Maybe because when I arrived to a *terreiro*, I had already known and performed some practices from Tantric Buddhism and from Padmasambhava in particular. For this reason, I started to establish a relationship with these spirits in a different way, and I began to feel that they were misunderstood, and also considered in a very limited manner.

This is something that, as we will see, also happened in the Tibetan culture, inside Hinduism and in Buddhism in particular, with some spirits who share the same characteristics with the Exus. Within this group of beings we can find spirits named, in some traditions, as *dakinis*.

TRAVELLERS OF THE THREE REALMS

The spirits called dakinis are, themselves, controversial and polemic, and unlike some of the simplistic interpretations of the term, their characteristics are diverse. Their manifestations are of different types and purposes, and the qualities that define a dakini make these spirits equivalent to those who in afro-Brazilian cults are known as pombagiras.

The concept of the dakini has been in a process of transformation and evolution since the first mentions appeared in ancient Hindu texts. This process can be observed inside Hindu culture itself, in which we can appreciate a change of perspective with the rise of the Tantrism for example, and then, when it arrived in Tibet, through Buddhism.

For example, in *The Tibetan Book of the Dead*, we find that a dakini is a female Yogini who has attained mundane and supramundane spiritual accomplishments (*siddhis*). They may be a human being who achieved such attainments, or they may be manifestations of the enlightened activity of some deities. The Tibetan equivalent is *mkha'gro ma*, which literally means "space voyager". Metaphorically space means emptiness, and voyager alludes to someone immersed in this experience. It is said that the teacher confers blessings, the meditational deity confers accomplishments, and the dakini is responsible for enlightenment.

Referring to magical practices, the Tibetan culture is particularly rich. Something to keep in mind is that when we study the appreciation and development of what is considered magic in Tibet, we have to try to abandon the vision that we have as occidental people related to magic, which is basically influenced by Christianity. To the Tibetans, and to the oriental culture in general, a separation does not exist between a material world – which is ruled by mundane affairs – and the world of the spirits. Instead, there is a constant interaction between them, an interaction at such a level that the separation we are accustomed to becomes deluded. So, in this way, it is common for example to invoke Kurukulle (also recognized as a dakini in some lineages and who is very popular among Tibetan people) to obtain a better job, to influence a boss, to give us an increase in our salary, to recover health, for the signing of a contract, or to obtain the reciprocity of somebody with whom we are in love.

Those are basically the fields in which a pombagira also acts, but, in my opinion, our relationship with this kind of spirit is yet very lacking, and we are far from visualizing and valorizing them in their entire dimension. It is lacking in the sense that we have strongly marked a separation between the material world and the spiritual one and, because of that, we generally try to obtain favors from somebody "from the other world", but who knows our world, by asking them to "descend" and help us. This is the product of the syncretism between the African cults and the Christian beliefs that predominates in our occidental culture. Lacking, moreover, because we have been accustomed to identifying demons and underworld spirits with something negative, diabolic, or with evil beings from the low astral that must be neutralized or avoided.

In the Vajrayana tradition for instance, we also find practices and prayers that are used before starting an activity in order to have a successful performance or to improve our health. There are some practices related to specific deities, which also implies issues like increasing our personal power, to develop our magnetism, or to obtain the blessing of beings who rule the elements, etc. One of the deities most popular for this matter in Tibet is Kurukulle, performing the role of a powerful, fully enlightened dakini who is capable of manifesting in different ways. We can find an example of this in this fragment of a prayer used to magnetize the world of appearances and possibilities, from the Chagdud Gompa tradition in the Nyingma lineage:

> Kurukulle, who captivates the mind of all who exist, without exception, you are rich with the power of the common signs and the sublime ones, and dances in ecstasy and vacuity. Legions of dakasvajra and dakinis that executed the power activities in the sphere of

supreme equality, the union between the appearance and vacuity, you make that the three spheres of the conditioned existence tremble with the dance of your vajra forms. You intimate the three realms with the sound of your laughter, your incessant illuminated speech...

Many things can be said about this fragment, but an important thing to emphasize is the constant display of opposites. We see that a separation or grade of valuation between the different realms does not exist, since the Vajra Consciousness arises as a product of the conjunction of all of them. It does not matter at what level the practitioner is; the activity of the dakini as a messenger and facilitator of knowledge is always present. One of her duties is to liberate the path of the practitioner from the obstacles caused by negative karma and the erroneous understanding of the nature of all things. Their way of action is like an "attack" on the illusory mind with illusion.

Some researchers have postulated the paradoxical character that the concept of dakini represents, showing itself as inaccessible from a rational point of view. In my opinion, the conception of pombagira represents this ambiguity, this impossibility of definition. It is not the purpose of this work to develop, in a deeper way, this point, which is a very interesting matter from the philosophical point of view and mystical as well, but to present the main aspects that led me to establish a syncretic relation between these spirits. One of the most important of these aspects is the quality of inaccessibility to the conceptual mind that the pombagira is and, at the same time, the profound reality that she represents through direct experience. Besides this, it is my intention to emphasize the function of the pombagira as a link, as a bridge between the illusory reality and the transcendental knowledge, between the full and the vacuous.

Everything that our perception shows as if it was stable and permanent, believing in its inner reality, are convictions that start to tremble and fall when we establish contact with a dakini. They have the key of the sublime wisdom but also of the mundane one, and this is precisely the quality that makes them messengers of the sublime. They incarnate the principle that the mundane and the sublime constantly interact, and all *siddhis* or accomplishments come through this interaction.

Maybe for most, it could be a little bit risky to establish a connection between a spirit who mostly appears in Kimbanda Terreiros and a well-known figure in the Hindu tradition as well as in the Buddhist environment, as it is with the dakini. But in particular, the figure and function of Maria Padilha in my life, joined with my familiarity with oriental traditions, made me raise my eyes beyond what could be considered "the possible", and open my mind to different and deeper possibilities.

I have found that there exists two great groups of spirits, those who were human and have reached sublime siddhis (accomplishment) and those who have never had a human manifestation. The first ones are known in the African tradition as *Egunes*. The dakinis take part of both categories, as we will see, and they are also considered as mediators, teachers and guides, without whom the ultimate realization cannot be achieved. These characteristics are, exactly, what I observe in Maria Padilha Queen of the Souls.

The dakinis represent the active energy in a feminine form, that which moves and nourishes. They can be guardians or protectors of sacred instructions or temples. We can find them in the water or muddy water, in the roads, as gatekeepers, in cemeteries, etc. There are dakinis who rule the elements, and in this way we have dakinis of the fire, of the earth, of the air, and ruling the water. They are related to different types of doctrines and in many cases they are responsible for the transmission of them. Among the traditions with a tantric base, it is said that it is not possible to achieve the Vajra State or the complete realization of the Self without the intervention of a dakini. They usually appear in a dancing form, or as constantly moving, because this represents our mundane mind, our attachment to the phenomenal world and, at the same time, it refers to the real nature of mind emerging from the phenomenal existence.

Reading the anthropologist and Kimbanda-initiate Nicholaj de Mattos Frisvold, we find that he describes pombagiras using words like ecstasies, cruelty, abuse, pleasure, and that we can find them in cemeteries, cabarets, taverns, in the street... The way that he describes them makes me think of some approaches that describe the dakinis as seductive sorceresses, dancing and powerful.

> Pombagira is a celebration of female virtue and power. In her we find a host of mighty rivers revealing how woman challenged the world. She is the vixen, the fornicator, the seducer, the revolutionary, the witch, the comforter, the lover, the concubine, the confidante, the queen and the saint. She is woman throughout time, mundane and mythical. She represents a particular refrain of characters and situations that add layer until we have a deep understanding of this voluptuous and intriguing woman. It is crucial that we realize that these refrains reveal her and are not something we ought to limit her by. Rather, they serve as examples of how the spirit of Pombagira acts upon the world and what forms of movements it creates. (de Mattos Frisvold, Nicholaj. *Pomba Gira and the Quimbanda of Mbùmba Nzila*. p. 33.)

Meanwhile, Per Kvaerne says about dakinis:

> The dakinis – whatever their ultimate origins outside the Land of Snow – are the 'fairies' of Tibet. They assume different forms and shapes, appearing as beautiful, smiling damsels, clad only in garlands carved from human bones; as old, toothless hags; or as ordinary human women of flesh and blood. Above all, they appear in visions and dreams, but whatever their guise, they are inspiratory, revealers of hidden treasures and transmitters of secret doctrines. (Kvaerne, Per. *The Bon Religion of Tibet*. p. 116.)

Sarah Harding expresses the following:

The idealized image of a female messenger, awesome keeper of the great mysteries to be revealed only to the deserving spiritual virtuoso, is packed with power and intrigue for both male and female practitioners. Though unique in its particulars to Himalayan Buddhism, it is found in reminiscent forms throughout the cultures and religions of the world. The mystery of the dakini herself will not be revealed because she is the very definition of mystery, and were she discovered by those other than mystics, it would not be she. (Harding, Sarah. *Niguma, Lady of Illusion.* p. 2.)

The drumming and dancing are both elements that pombagiras use to manifest themselves with different purposes. Dancing, for example, is not just a simple group of sensual movements, but a style of energetic handling that leads to a specific kind of energy or knowledge that has to be brought into that moment. Moreover, it has the purpose of stimulating the flux of energy through our channels. The conjunction of all of this prepares us for the highest levels of learning and understanding and, in some cases, for the depuration of emotional afflictions and all that is recorded in our energetic body.

Some scholars says that in Tibet, in pre-Buddhist times, many spirits or demons were satisfied and calmed through ritualistic sacrifices, and that in those ceremonies dancing was considered a way of moving energy. It used to be common that through those sacrifices, pacts and alliances were also established in order to obtain knowledge, protection, and mastery directly from the spirits. With the arrival of Buddhism, most of these rituals were partly transformed and adapted to the Buddhist Mahayana conception.

An example of this is what is known as the *Chod Ritual*, which literally means "Cutting Off". Mahayana Buddhism, and also the Vajrayana path, uses this ritual as a practice whose purpose is to destroy the mundane passions and the karmic effects. For some experts, the Chod Ritual would be the form that evolved from a kind of rite belonging to the pre-Buddhist era, in which it was usual to offer sacrifices to demons and underworld beings with the purpose of obtaining their help in mundane affairs as well as in one's inner spiritual development. Dancing was also performed, and was generally offered to the dakinis, who represented bridges between the spiritual world and the material one. They were the active energy, and for this reason they have the ability to eliminate erroneous conceptions.

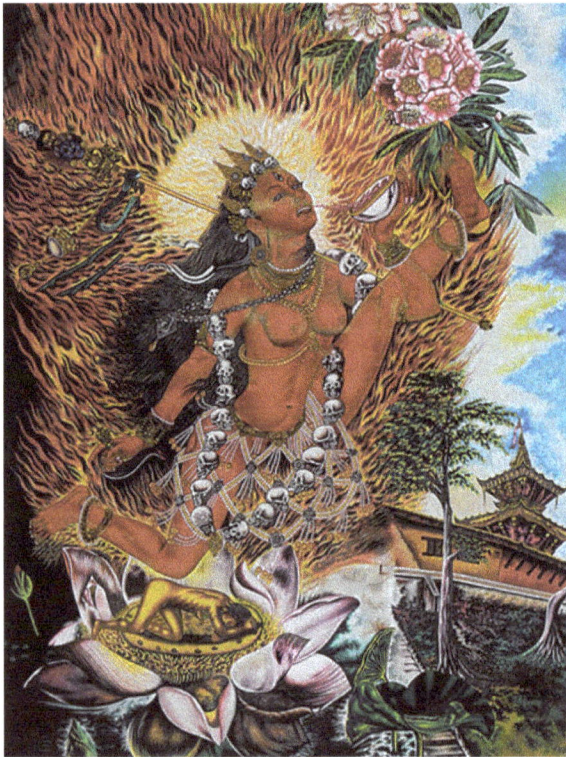

Vajra Yogini: That Mighty Wave of Passionate Commitment to Truth and Freedom, Tibetan Thangka Painting

The word dakini does not have a specific translation, or concrete attributes. Scholars who have deeply investigated this topic affirm that it is a term that, while maintaining some similarities, has been changed in its meaning throughout the Indian and Tibetan cultures in which it is used. Thus, Judith Simmer-Brown, in her book *Dakini's Warm Breath* says:

Dakini is a term derived from Indian regional Prakrit or possibly Sanskrit, vulgar in connotation, attributed to a minor player in the pantheon of deities associated with indigenous non-Brahmanical traditions of India. Dakinis were demonic inhabitors [sic] of cemeteries and charnel grounds, delighting in the taste of human flesh and blood and dancing with ornaments fashioned from the bones of decaying corpses. They were identified as witch-spirits of women who died in pregnancy or childbirth. Unfaithful wives were also suspected of becoming dakinis. When angered, these witches were capable of causing pestilence among humans, especially fever, obsessions, lung diseases and infertility. They were wrath personified, joining the slaughter on the battlefield, intoxicated from thirstily sucking the blood of their victims... (Simmer-Brown, Judith. *Dakini's Warm Breath: The Feminine Principle in Tibetan Buddhism*. p. 45.)

Meanwhile, Miranda Shaw says:

Anyone who reads a Tantric text or enters a Tantric temple immediately encounters a dazzling array of striking female imagery. One discovers a pantheon of female Buddhas and a host of female enlighteners known as dakinis. The dakinis leap and fly, unfettered by clothing, encircled by billowing hair, their bodies curved in sinuous dance poses. Their eyes blaze with passion, ecstasy, and ferocious intensity. One can almost hear the soft clacking of their intricate bone jewelry... Expressions of the motif in Tantric literature describe yoginis with magical powers, powerful enchantresses with the ability to change shape at will, and enlightened women who can spark a direct experience of reality with a precisely aimed word or gesture. (Shaw, Miranda. *Passionate Enlightenment.* p. 3.)

Dakinis can be seen as wrathful and terrible manifestations or as peaceful and pleasant ones. We can interpret this as the dark and the light side. In the Hindu mythology, dakinis are associated with the Goddess Kali and also with Goddess Durga.

It is said that Durga was created with the purpose of defeating the Asuras, whom nobody could kill because they were an almost invincible army. She liberated innumerable feminine warriors whose characteristics were depravation, lust, and the desire for flesh and blood. She succeeded in making them use those characteristics for the benefit of the Supreme. They fought incessantly until they overcame and consumed the demon by sucking his blood. The text where this myth is told is part of the Mandukya Purana. It is also said that many animals were sacrificed in order that the goddess would fulfill her task. This is one example of beings that could be considered as dakinis, acting as a kind of messenger for a divinity.

In relation to Kali, the dakinis perform divine tasks as well as worldly ones, and many times they appear in very frightening ways. They also fulfill the duty of leading the dead to the Underworld. They can be found at cemeteries, places of death, and fields of battle. They are completely related to death in a very wide way, and with blood. In different periods in India, the term dakini was interpreted with different connotations: as messengers, spirits guides, and mediators, but also as tricksters and witches. They were also called "she-devils" by the first western scholars who started to become interested in Tibet and India; an example of this is Lawrence Waddell.[61]

---

61. "Those who permanently adopt the hermit life are called the "packed-up ones", and those of the highest rank are "the great recluses".

The word dakini in the Hindu society, as well as in the Tibetan, designated women who perform practices prohibited by society: prostitution, and crimes. It was also appointed to those women who were unfaithful to their husbands, or who used to behave against society's rules. Some women were called "dakinis" because they were priestesses of a divinity whose cult was prohibited, or because they performed activities related to death or to the profane. The rise of Tantrism offered a new approach to the way that some spirits were treated and in certain practices rescued pre-Brahamanic traditions, but in many sectors of the society, things have not changed so much. Even nowadays, in the Hindu and Tibetan societies, the profound and sacred meaning of the word dakini is unfamiliar, and is still associated with spirits of low astral and with women of "doubtful" reputation, those dedicated to the delight of men or to witchcraft. This is another point of convergence between the dakinis and the pombagiras. Until now in our societies, thanks to the ingenuous Kardecist vision, pombagiras were treated and seen as dark spirits of the low astral, only devoted to fulfilling mundane or egocentric tasks.

In Vajrayana Buddhism, the dakinis perform many roles and have many classifications. As our present purpose is to set off the predominant notes that led me to establish the nexus between dakinis and pombagiras, we are going to divide them in a more general way, into two great groups: the mundane or worldly dakinis, and the fully enlightened dakinis.

The Mundane or Worldly Dakini generally denotes those feminine spirits that were called demons in pre-tantric traditions. They can achieve great levels of power in magical practices, and they are a great help to practitioners if they recognize them and know how to deal with them. But, they can also put their knowledge in service of low purposes; they can show themselves in a hostile and malevolent way, representing great obstacles. For them, our intentions and our goals are crucial.

They are engaged in ascetic exercises and are usually followers of the Vajruyuna system, seeking Siddhi and its wizard powers by the aid of the Dakkini she-devils and the king-devils who are their tutelaries." Waddell, Lawrence Austine. *The Buddhism of Tibet.* p. 352.

The important thing here is not to find a way of avoiding them, but to learn how to treat and to work with them, as they could be great sources of knowledge. Some of them serve high purposes, or they are messengers of fully enlightened beings. Their contribution to the spiritual path is very worthy, because they are fast assistants in the removal of obstacles in the daily practice, and through this, the Worldly Dakinis achieve the state of a fully enlightened being.

The Wisdom Dakini is a very important spiritual entity and a key to understanding Vajrayana Buddhism as well as the Tantric traditions. They represent the enlightened mind, beyond any concept of gender. They are the symbol of the mind *par excellence*. The phenomenal world and its transcendence are represented by them. Recognizing them in their most elevated manifestation requires a great training of the mind. It is said that the great yogi and magician Padmasambhava, the father of Tantric Buddhism, received the highest empowerments from a dakini, but the first time that she appeared to him, he did not recognize her.[62]

---

62. "When the great Yogin Padmasambhava, called by Tibetans Guru Rinpoche, "the precious teacher", embarks on his spiritual journey, he travels from place to place requesting teachings from yogins and yoginis. Guided by visions and dreams, his journey takes him to desolate forests populated with ferocious wild animals, to poison lakes with fortified islands, and to cremation grounds. [...] When he hears of the supreme queen of all dakinis, the greatly accomplished yogini called Secret Wisdom, he travels to the Sandal Grove cremation ground to the gates of her abode, the Palace of Skulls. He attempts to send a request to the queen with her maidservant Kumari. But the girl ignores him and continues to carry huge brass jugs of water suspended from a heavy yoke across her shoulders. When he presses his request, Kumari continues her labors, remaining silent. The great yogin becomes impatient and, through his yogic powers, magically nails the heavy jugs to the floor. No matter how hard Kumari struggles, she cannot lift them.

Removing the yoke and ropes from her shoulders, she steps before Padmasambhava, exclaiming, "You have developed great yogic powers. What of my powers, great one?" And so saying, she draws a sparkling crystal knife from the girdle at her waist and slices open her heart center, revealing the vivid and vast interior space of her body.[...] Abashed that he did not realize with whom he was dealing, Guru Rinpoche bows before her and humbly renews his request for teachings."[...] Simmer-Brown, Judith. *Dakini's Warm Breath*, pp.1-2.

Something important to emphasize is that in the Hindu tradition, the different categories of dakinis and the tasks that they perform are differentiated more clearly, something that does not occur in the Tibetan tradition, where most of the time the dakinis exchange aspects and duties in a dynamic display. Sometimes, a mundane dakini appears as a wisdom dakini, and vice versa. Recognizing the type of spirit that we have in front of us and its purpose is of fundamental importance in the Tantric path. For this, the purification practices and the training of the mind are indispensable, and also practices to equilibrate the elements within us. Even this is not a common practice among the Kimbanda practitioners in Brazil; my contacts with Maria Padilha Queen of the Souls confirmed that, and she made me feel that it is an essential condition to establish a profound contact with her, and to penetrate and understand the Exu dimension. Let us see what some authors say about this:

> In her manifestation as a flesh-eating demoness, she may be acting on behalf of negative forces opposed to spirituality. She may be an attendant force, acting as a protect aide [sic] to her liege, who may be a realized being or merely a powerful shaman. Or she may be fully realized herself, acting as a teacher, messenger or protector of the dharma. (Simmer-Brown, Judith, *Dakini's Warm Breath.* p. 54.)

> In general the dakini represents the ever changing flow of energy with which the yogic practitioner must work in order to become realized. She may appear as a human being, as a goddess – either peaceful or wrathful – or she may be perceived as the general play of energy in the phenomenal world. (Tsultrim, Allione. *Women of Wisdom.* p. 103.)

Exu is the divine messenger, he represents the principle of movement, of indetermination, he is a link, a connection. He represents the union between the spiritual world and the material one and, for this reason, without him the possibility of spiritual knowledge would not exist. Exu is the gatekeeper, and this characteristic can manifest in the material world, giving to us the material or economic means to obtain a suitable position in order to dedicate us to spiritual things. Exu also keeps the key of wisdom; it is through our contact with him that our spiritual path really starts. Without Exu nothing can be done, in the same way that without the dakini, nothing can be achieved. In all traditions that are based on the possibility of full accomplishment, there exists an entity, a spirit, which has the same characteristics as Exu.

Exu, as well as the kingdom of dakas and dakinis, is a protector, the guardian of the Law. There exists a Law, a principle, a syntony through which the Universe vibrates and manifests itself. Micro-cosmos and Macro-cosmos intercept each other showing the immanent quality of non-duality, and entities like Exu, dakas, dakinis, establish and represent by themselves this nexus, this point of union.

As with the dakinis, the pombagira is, herself, a symbolic element that oscilates between what she suggests and what she represents. Her dance or "gira" reveals the perception of our mundane mind in relation to the Universe, which is an enigma for our understanding. We discover a new dimension, and experience a breakdown of all our convictions. Working with the pombagira is a difficult work of perception and the forthcoming of a deep reality – it is a diving into this new reality. Pombagira is also the experience of the illusory, which is impossible to transcend without these experiences.

The dwelling of Exu is the crossroads, the cemetery, the roads. They are places that represent change, a place of encounter between the human and the divine, where opposites meet each other, where a decision must be taken. They are also places synonymous of death – of death not as loss, but as the inevitable change from which something will be born. Death is understood as the constant elements of dance, of their action and interaction. We are always life, but we are always death at the same time.

In some of the Oriental traditions, no condemnation against what we can call the dark side of our consciousness exists, and to reach the Vajra State does not mean that our dark side must disappear, or "transform into light" as we usually read in the New Age spiritualist speeches, but to understand that one emerges from the other. The Vajra state means "beyond the duality", which means to amalgamate what seems to be detached. In this way, the symbolism of the dakinis is very rich in expressions of the underworld, of demoniacal beings, of wrathful deities, of sumptuous women showing their sexuality and eternal youth, bodies semi-naked or naked, and the constant mention of blood, in some cases menstrual blood, as a representation of life. We also see reflected in them the compassionate and serene expression of knowledge, for they are the fast saviors who help practitioners on their paths.

It is very interesting to notice that the iconography, the style in which pombagiras and dakinis are represented visually, has many points in common. Elements like skulls, roses, blood, tridents, knives or daggers, phurbas[63], and colors like red, black, and white are predominant. The murmurs and the loud laughter are also characteristics of both of them. Those iconographic details could be widely examined, but for the purpose of this work we will just note that these are elements which appeared in antique texts about tantric practices of Tibetan Buddhism, mostly those inherited from the Bon Tradition. June Campbell says that elements of ritualistic uses like skulls and even the uses of blood were an important part of some specific tantric rituals to attain liberation in a single life. She says that that rituals were maintained in secret and only a few could learn about them. Other researchers sustain that these practices (which involve the uses of skulls, blood, and ritualistic

---

63. The phurba has a very deep meaning and is linked to certain deities especially in its wrathful manifestations, but as mere information we can say that it is a kind of ritual dagger, considered a powerful tool that cuts and destroys negative energies and the negative action of our own mental poisons, creating a kind of protective field for the practitioner. It can be made of different materials like bone, metal, wood, crystal, etc., and it should be consecrated to fulfill its purpose.

sacrifices) were not part of the ancient tantrism, but could have been introduced from Iran, western Asia, and China.[64]

María Padilha Queen of the Souls is almost always represented with a skull near her feet or in her hands. From my point of view, this not only represents the kingdom of the dead, but also the vacuity inherent in all material existence. The vacuity of our reality and that all that we perceive as immutable is nothing more than the illusory perception of our mind.

The nature of the dakinis is, as with Exu, tricky. Most of the time, their teachings proceed by proofs, challenges, or the dakinis themselves appear in tempting or frightening forms (shapes) in order to test the practitioner. Their skill is also to make communicable their knowledge, even though always in a symbolic way. The feminine manifestation of Exu is the pombagira, who embodies the duty of teacher, source and giver of instructions.

The way that we see and perceive what surrounds us, all that happens to us, and even ourselves depends on our state of mind. I am not talking about the process of evolution to which the Kardecists referred, but a process of cleanliness, clarification, and calming (stillness) of our mental processes. The function of the pombagira as a guide, as the active cause of knowledge, is only revealed when our thoughts calm down and our mind becomes more clear and apprehensive. It is in that moment that the dakini function appears to us, that we can see her beyond her attributes, that we are able to recognize more than her appearance or manifested form. Without this process, we just see a feminine spirit in which we deposit all of our expectations; we see in her all that is repressed by the society from which we come, by our families, by

---

64. "The skull is equally important in Tantric Buddhist rituals. Not only is it carried by many deities (including the dakini) as a skull-cup, topa (Tibetan thod.pa; Sanskrit kapala), filled with blood or amrita (the fluid of life), but it is also filled during certain rituals with fluids which symbolize menstrual blood, semen, urine, faeces or saliva, which are then made as offerings to wrathful deities. These practices can also be found in Bon rituals and are in all likelihood linked to the shamanistic practices which once were spread from the Atlantic to the Pacific." *Traveller in Space: Gender, identity and Tibetan Buddhism*. June Campbell. Ed. Continuum. p. 43.

our cultures. We see her attached to mundane form, and we can only work with her in this way.

This new form of relationship with a pombagira arose to me after my initiation in the Vajrayana path, and it was specifically with Maria Padilha Queen of the Souls, to whom this work is dedicated.

Maria Padilha Queen of the Souls embodies an active and eternal principle; she also represents the dissolution of the five elements. Her presence, her iconography related to cemeteries and to death, represents, in a more elevated sense, dissolution, transcendence, and emptiness. Although she also embodies the principles of lust, desire, and amorality, she is the disintegration of all that. It is because of this that we can call her "the cause of knowledge". In the same way as a dakini, she is the protector of the paths, the guardian of instructions and of empowerments; she is death and life without ending or beginning. She represents, through her dance, the phenomenal world in permanent change.

During my research for this work, I found a poem named "The Crimson Rose Skydancer"[65], dedicated to the Red Dakini. I feel that it condenses all we have been talking about in a very strong and delicate manner. I immediately thought of Maria Padilha Queen of the Souls, her delicacy as well as her ferocity. It was in this way that I first saw her. These are some fragments of the poem:

I am the Vajra Dakini, of light the color of crimson roses and flowing blood

I transmute the life energies into their spiritual origin

By filtering out gross elements and giving them form

By changing weak currents into strong ones, dribbling energy into pounding waves.

Opening blocks and barriers so that pain and pleasure may be experienced in their full strength.

I cause dry channels to become full, dying plants to become lush (...)

(...) I am the guide and introducer of men to the spiritual path

---

65. "The Crimson Rose Skydancer" was written by a Buddhist practitioner who wishes to remain anonymous. It is used here with the author's permission.

I strengthen and purify them that they may encounter the great Buddhas of Light

I prepare them for the Great Awakening (...)

(...) I act as teacher as well as dancer (...)

(...)I harmonize the spiritual striving of all beings

I call them forth, into the realms of the enlightened ones

That they may pass through the dangerous waters

To watch the rising of the sun upon the other shore

Blessing of the roses of passionate love (...)

A Practical Approach

The way that we perceive the manifestation and energy of the spirits depends on our own grade of development, degree of internal purification, and the stillness of our mind. Our environment, our being-in-the-world, is a perfect reflection of the state of our minds. When we decide to perform certain magical practices or to work with spirits, we must know that the state of our mind is crucial. We should prepare our mind and our body first, in order to obtain a calm mind and a strong body capable of receiving the energies. It is good to train in disciplines that lead us to a state of correspondence and union between our body and mind. For this reason, meditation or a technique like Yoga or Chi Kung should be an essential part of the magical practitioner's path.

We have different ways of establishing contact with a spirit. We are spiritual beings who also have a material existence; according to this, contact with other spirits is a natural thing. However, we learn to forget this through our life experience, maybe because we are told that spirits are diabolical things, and that diabolical things are related to perversion and to evil, and that to try to go beyond our human nature is sign of pride and one of the greatest sins. Western societies are highly molded by Christianity and for this reason, we become accustomed to the idea that to be in contact with spirit is something wrong, something that deserves punishment. Even if we do not hold those beliefs anymore, our mind has grown accustomed to them, and they have become a kind of program that still functions in our unconscious mind. We need to reestablish our link with the spiritual world and leave aside the idea that working with energy is something strange, something belonging to some chosen one.

Worship and invocation lead us to live magic as a natural thing; it is why they are so important. Spirits do not belong to any specific religion or spiritual path, they take part in different realms and they work according to different purposes. All of them, without exception, have things to teach us. For this reason, it is important to treat them with respect, and to have confidence in our own guides, and again, the more calm our mind becomes, the greater are our improvements, our work, and our comprehension of our real purpose.

The first time I got in touch with the energy of Maria Padilha Queen of the Souls, as I said at the beginning of this work, was in a Kimbanda *Terreiro*. When I saw her for the first time, I felt an enormous connection with her – something very deep inside me awoke. In some way, many of my questions were answered. After I left that *Terreiro*, I continued worshipping her in my own way. I used to light candles and incense for her and to pray – nothing standard, simply the words that I felt in the moment.

The first time I went to Brazil, with the man who is now my husband, I asked him to take me to a cemetery to offer roses for my Lady (as I used to call her). We found a very old cemetery on an island, in Rio de Janeiro. It is very difficult to find a cemetery in Brazil that is open during the night, but I found it. It was almost midnight, the entry gate was totally open and there was nobody around, not even in the street. I entered, and I left seven red roses and one white on a grave that I felt was suitable. I closed my eyes and I called to her, saying, "Thank you for being my guide, my master... thank you for protecting my back". I prayed to her with the words that appeared in my mind. Immediately, I heard a murmur, and for an instant a soft breeze wrapped around me. I knew that she was there and had received my offering. The experience was amazing!

Recently, I began to invoke her in a different way, using techniques that I learned among the Vajrayana teachings...and she responded. I started to feel her energy in different ways and for different purposes. I started to feel that she could put me in touch with the active part of the instructions, and so I discovered that she is what in Tibetan terms is called a dakini. She has acted as a remover of obstacles; she has improved my energy, my resistance, and my health. She has also guided me to profound meditational experiences, and shown me how to recognize the mental state that must be left aside in order to make progress on the spiritual path.

Maria is passing through a process of transformation. I prefer to use the word "transformation" instead of "evolution", because I feel that spiritual energy is better described through the property of transformation. We know that what sometimes describes the qualities of Exu itself is movement and change, but the process that I am making reference to is of another type – I think that she is achieving the supreme *siddhis* (accomplishments).

Since I first saw her, she has shown herself as a spirit of great knowledge. She has mastered many techniques that could lead you to the highest levels if you are capable of understand her symbolic language.

I would like to clarify that I am not against working with Exu for mundane purposes, such as obtaining a good job or to improve your life in different ways; we are also material beings with material needs. I would simply propose that another kind of work is also possible. Maybe a more complete work, because in changing the way that our mind operates, we change all of our life experiences. If we want to live magic, we need to work in a more complete way.

We do not have a light side opposed to a dark side; we have complementary sides, and spirits from different realms. A considerable part of Maria's teaching is directed to showing and demonstrating this. We must learn to manage in different dimensions and with different kinds of beings.

Since we started to establish contact with an entity such as Maria, we have perceived what we can call an evolutionary line – evolution in the sense that through the invocations, our contact started to change in intensity and form. But an indispensable condition is the purification practices that we perform, the frequency with which we perform them, and our energetic alignment.

Two years ago, I read a book by Christopher Penczak in which Reiki was related to practical magic. Reiki was used as a way of achieving alignment of the body, and as a way of preparing the atmosphere for ritual. For me it was a great discovery, because, since I had received all my Traditional Usui Reiki attunements, including the Master attunement, I felt that there was a strong connection between Reiki and the work with spirits. That book was the confirmation of that belief, and I started to use Reiki in that way, in my personal alignment, in the preparation of the room, and as a meditational and purification practice.

In this way, techniques like Reiki and some others coming from the Vajrayana tradition prepare us for a more intense contact with the entities, because they have the ability to clean our energetic channels and to calm our mind to a deep understanding. Yoga is also of great help. During my invocation to Maria, she showed me the importance of those activities as well as a healthy style of life. She advised me to be aware of myself, my emotions, and even my food.

There have been three tools that led me to develop this new way of contact with Maria Padilha Queen of the Souls: academic study (mainly all things related to different traditions based on contact and apprenticeship with spirit), Reiki, and Guru Yoga.

But, I must confess that I became a little bit impressed by the inclusion of Reiki in this type of practice, because even I have always felt Reiki as something more than a simple healing technique, though most of its practitioners talk about it in relation to health or to overcoming stress. I started to research even more deeply on the subject, and the answer arrived a few years later. In a recent book, Frank Arjava Petter, one of the most renowned Reiki Master and researchers about the topic, says:

> A Miko is a woman who understand the voice of the Gods. She is able to communicate with the souls of the dead, and in a state of trance she serves as a mediator between the gods and the humans. All Japanese Reiki sources talk about the aim for the practitioner to become like a miko. He/she is to rely on the sky and let himself be guided by the gods. (*This is Reiki*. Frank Arjava Petter. Kindle Edition.)

This interpretation is derived from the analysis of the ancient characters that compound the ideogram of the word Reiki. Japanese society has always been involved with the cult of their ancestors and for this reason, it is easy to agree with Arjava Petter and to see Reiki as a practice related to the kingdom of the spirits.

Nowadays, perhaps, we have become accustomed to the New Age version, related to harmonization. But actually, the ultimate goal of the practitioner, if we consider Reiki at its source, is to hear the voice of the spirit, to hear the voice of the ancestors and the gods, in order to ask for their intervention.

Reiki, as a complete system of harmonization, cleanses our energetic channels and balances them at the same time. Reiki makes us more sensitive to energy, from our surroundings to ourselves, and gives us the ability to recognize our energetic state and our mental processes, and helps us to have an effect on them.

Guru Yoga is a technique whose function is to merge our mind with the wisdom mind, represented by our guru or guide. It helps us to make good use of the information that we receive. It is a kind of tool that permits us a good understanding of the symbolic language of the dakinis. It is the practice that opens the doors to the highest level attunements, because it expands our consciousness.

Certainly there exists similar practices in other magical systems or doctrines that lead us to the same result. Maria advised me to make of Guru Yoga a habitual practice, maybe because of my familiarity with the technique, or because I had received the empowerment of Guru Yoga a few years before.

Contact with her can be received in different ways, including physical sensations. The periodic realization of the ritual of invocation produces an increase in our capacity to communicate with her and with other similar spirits. It is progressive preparation to different levels and stages.

Allione Tsultrim, talking about the dakini, says the following:

> By consciously invoking the dakini through Tantric practices we begin to develop sensitivity to energy itself. When looking at the iconography of the dakini we should bear in mind that through understanding her symbols and identifying with her, we are identifying with our own energy. (Tsultrim, Allione. *Women of Wisdom.* p. 107.)

It is necessary to perform our ritual in a place where we cannot be interrupted and where we can stay as long as necessary.

Something to keep in mind is that the effectiveness of the invocation does not depend on its duration, because one of its purposes is to open new doors of knowledge, to amplify our perception to higher levels.

We can prepare the environment using fumigation (I personally like Myrrh), candles (it is better to start with white ones), and cleansing our energetic body (we can use Reiki or another similar technique). She can be called through a *ponto riscado*, through a prayer that we can say at any moment, from our hearts, invoking her attributes. The key is to remain quiet, paying attention to our breath with our mind open and calm. The real communication with her starts when we are prepared; for this reason, we have to be patient and persistent, leaving aside all expectations.

Of course we can perform the invocation with a question in mind, something that we would like to learn or achieve, but, in this case, express it with your intentions and then free it. We do not stay stuck on the subject, because we could miss other important things that may appear which could be the preparation for what we want.

Another important thing is to pay attention in our daily life. Our entire life is a magical display, and spirits who are messengers and intermediaries teach through the most unexpected things. We must be aware of any kinds of signals, such as dreams, words that come to mind, something that somebody says, emotional states, etc.

It is essential to remain firm, and to be confident in our guide. Maria is a spirit of high wisdom who can lead us with safety through different realms, and who knows our limitations and fears as human beings. From my point of view, it is better to start with a simple invocation, a simple work in order to become accustomed with the energy and to make a deeper contact with the spirit. After that, she is who is going to lead us. But, we must remember that nothing is more powerful than a strong invocation, one with confidence and, perhaps, without words.

Some pages previous, we said that to recognize and attain the non-duality state, or our complete realization, is necessary to establish a deep contact with the essence of the pombagira, that is, to enter into a new dimension, the Exu dimension. It is different from any experience that we could have before; it is a complete mystery in which we find ourselves alone in front of a reality that, at the beginning, exceeds us completely. But it is not because we are inferior or for lack of conditioning; it is because we are not accustomed to handling the darkness, with its incessant change, because the Kingdom of Exu is, in itself, the impermanence. Exu represents the impermanence and, at the same time, its overcoming.

If we want to attain the non-duality state, we must enter into this mysterious and unknown kingdom, we must penetrate it and understand it, reaching a comprehension about its laws and how they work.

Once we have established our first contact with it, we cannot turn around. Our only possibility is to continue. All in our life begins to change; our perceptions and our convictions are shaken. This is a dark kingdom that put us face to face with our own darkness, with all the things that we ignore and fear. We must understand this process as a rebirth, but sometimes, depending on our state of mind and our training, the process can be very difficult and painful.

A powerful oracle that I had the privilege to hear a few days before writing this, revealed that if we want to understand life, we must understand death; to walk hand in hand with life, we must also walk with death. One is not present without the other. The Exu Kingdom is the door that leads to that comprehension. We are accustomed to managing with duality, but we are far from understanding it properly, because we want to control everything and we become extremely attached to the comfortable part of our lives.

But here, the figure of the pombagira represents the torch that shows us the path to follow. We are light, but we are shadow too, and at the bottom of our hearts, we are extremely fearful of our own shadow, because it represents what is beyond our control. But real magic, as a practical science, belongs to the shadow, and we can learn and develop techniques that can help us to understand and manage this "dark" side. We start to establish a relationship with spirits that can help or teach us in our journey, through invocations, pacts, and alliances. Pombagiras have the duty of being the cause of knowledge, of putting us in touch with the source of everything. They are the darkness and they are the torch.

Great Lady of Darkness,
You Who appears in the deepest night
You Who are the cause and source of all knowledge,
Being the occult and the visible
The sacred and the profane....
You Who shows the flame of the perfect and intrinsic wisdom,
by Yourself reached and sustained....
You who possesses the magnificent secret treasure,
Key of all doors and of all fulfillment...
It is You to whom I give homage in the crossroads of my soul,
It is your steps and your torch that I look for in my thorny path.
It is your rod that leads in the gloomy spaces of my being....

To You I dedicate this work, as well I put my life at
your entire service...It is an honor to walk with You
and to be your priestess.... Honor to which I aspire
to serve with the greatest fortitude and devotion....

Praised and worshipped be,
Lady and Queen of the Crossroads....
Maria Padilha of the Souls!

BIBLIOGRAPHY

Anon. "Red Dakini." Buddha Nature. N.p., n.d. Web. <http://www.buddhanature.com/buddha/vajradakini.html>.

Arjava Peter, Frank. *This is Reiki*. Lotus Press Shangri-la, USA, 2012. [Kindle Edition].

Asante, Molefi Kete and Mazama, Ed. *Encyclopedia of African Religion*. Sage Publication, Inc, 2009.

Bethencourt, Francisco. *O Imaginário da Magia*. Schwarcz. 2004.

Campbell, June. *Traveller in Space: Gender, Identity and Tibetan Buddhism*. Continuum. Revised edition. New York, USA, 2002.

Dakini, Red. "Welcome To a Celebration of the Female Spirit as Manifest in the Dakini." Dakini Land. N.p., 1 Nov. 2001. Web. <http://www.dakini.demon.co.uk/>.

de Mattos Frisvold, Nicholaj. *Pomba Gira and the Quimbanda of Mbùmba Nzila*. Scarlet Imprint, 2011.

Elbein dos Santos, Juana. *Os Nago e a Morte*. Vozes, Petrópolis, 1975, 13ª edition.

Harding, Sarah. *Niguma: Lady of Illusion*. Snow Lion Publications, New York, 2010.

Manmatha Nath Dutt. M.A., M.R.A.S, Trans. *Markandeya Puranam*. Kolkata.

Mipham, Jamgon. *White Lotus: an explanation of the Seven Line Prayer to Guru Rinpoche*. Shambala Publication, Inc. Boston, USA, 2007.

Kvarnae, Per. *The Bon Religion of Tibet: The Iconography of a Living Tradition*. Shambhala, Boston, 1996.

Reynolds, John Myrdhin. "Wisdom Dakinis, Passionate and Wrathful." Vajranatha.com. N.p., 29 Mar. 2009. Web. <http://vajranatha.com/teaching/Dakinis.htm>.

"Kurukulla: The Dakini of Magic and Enchantments." Vajranatha.com. N.p., 29 Mar. 2009. Web. <http://vajranatha.com/teaching/Kurukulla.htm>.

Simmer-Brown, Judith. *Dakini's Warm Breath: The Feminine Principle in Tibetan Buddhism.* Shambala Publication, Inc, Boston, 2001.

Shaw, Miranda. *Passionate Enlightenment: Women in Tantric Buddhism.* Princeton University Press, New Jersey, 1995.

Thupten, Jinpa and Coleman. *The Tibetan Book of the Dead: First Complete Translation.* Penguin Books Ltd., London, 2006.

Tsultrim, Allione. *Women of Wisdom.* Snow Lion Publications, Ithaca, USA, 2000.

Unknown. "Dakini." Khandro Net, n.d. Web. <http://www.khandro.net/dakini_khandro.htm>.

Waddell, Laurence Austine. *The Buddhism of Tibet.* WH Allen & CO, London. 1895.

Willis, Janice D. *Feminine Ground: Essays on Women and Tibet.* Snow Lion Publications. New York, 1995 (Second Edition).

INDEX

A.

ashè 60, 61

B.

Book of Saint Cyprian, The 11, 19, 43
Book of the Law, The 71
Buddhism 83, 91

C.

cabula 30, 31
calundu 29, 30
Cathedral of Seville 10, 13
Chod Ritual 83
crossroads 37, 64, 90

D.

dakini 78, 79
  iconography 91
  mundane 87
  red 93
  wisdom 88
dead, the 19, 39, 59, 98
  categories of 9, 11, 18, 81
  communication with 30
  offerings to 32, 60, 62
de Bourbon, Blanche 9, 10, 14, 15
de Castille, Enrique II 14
demons 58
  legions of 17, 58
  wives of 23, 39
    mentioned in spells 44
de Padilla, Maria. **See also** Maria Padhila 9, 42
  burial of 10

Q.

R.

S.

T.

U.

V.

W.

.